OPTIONS TRADING STRATEGIES

THE ULTIMATE AND COMPLETE GUIDE ON HOW TO MAKE MONEY WITH THE BEST AND WORKING OPTIONS TRADING STRATEGIES TO GENERATE A LONG-TERM PASSIVE INCOME AND QUIT YOUR JOB

ARTHUR D. RICHIE

Table of Contents

Introduction

By this stage, you have mastered all the basics as well as the most intermediate trading strategies. It is now time to delve deeper into more advanced strategies. You need to learn and understand several concepts before you eventually become a pro trader.

For instance, you need to understand the various options pricing models, why stock options act the way they do, volatility and how it affects markets, measuring options' sensitivity to underlying stock's movements, and so on. These are essential topics if you are to trade successfully and earn a decent passive income for many years.

You haven't be intimidated by these advanced strategies. While they may have a reputation for being complex and complicated, you should be willing to take the time and learn as much as possible. If you take your time and understand the concepts behind the different strategies and Spreads, you will soon become a pro. Also, many options traders agree that these strategies and techniques aren't that complex.

Take the Time to Learn

Since you want to skyrocket your income, it is important to learn about advanced options trading. There are definitions and terms and strategies, tools, techniques, and so much more. However, since you have come this far and have learned so much over the months and years, you can expect to fare very well. With the knowledge you acquire through this book, you will become an advanced trader who can trade all sorts of instruments, including futures, Forex, ETFs, binaries, and stocks. When you acquire this knowledge, you will achieve a much clearer understanding of how options behave and why they behave the way they do. This way, you will be able to explore the different scenarios in the market.

Learn How Strategies Work Step-by-Step

Also by this stage, you should be familiar with both fundamental analysis and technical analysis. Some traders choose one over the other, while others opt for both. After you have done your analysis, you determine which strategies to apply based on that analysis. Advanced options trading strategies closely resemble Putting together processes to achieve set objectives. You need to learn more about eliminating some strategies based on the outcomes of your analysis.

Flexibility

Advanced trading is more about the freedom and flexibility that you are exposed to. Once you enter a position, you will expect one of three things to happen, either long or short. These three things are upward price movement, downwards price movement, or no movements. The challenge here is that only one movement out of these possible three will result in a profit.

Fortunately, with advanced trading strategies, you can profit regardless of the conditions in the market. Should the price movement remain within a predetermined range, you will be guaranteed to make a profit. So, you will profit if the price moves up, profit if the price goes down, and you will be profitable should there be no price movement at all.

Freedom

Since there is a lot of flexibility with advanced options strategies, we also see plenty of freedom. A lot of people get caught up in either of these two categories. They would love to work hard and generate an income for their partners and loved ones. Sadly, most people have to work, which makes it impossible for them to trade regularly.

These individuals don't desire to trade daily and watch the markets every hour and even minute after minute. It can be tedious. It is where swing trading comes in handy. You can become a swing trader where you place trades and then go about your business for a couple more days.

Advanced Options Trading

You already understand how Put and Call options are traded on the markets and have had sufficient experience to advance your knowledge. By this stage, you should be ready to discover the amazing power of these options' flexibility and versatility through different advanced strategies.

Strategies

Options strategies can be defined as trading methods that use options in different combinations to produce market positions that enable traders to benefit regardless of the market conditions.

There are four major strategies when it comes to options. These strategies are bearish, bullish options strategies, volatile strategies, and neutral options strategies. Volatile strategies tend to profit when the market moves sharply in any direction or implied volatility increases.

Neutral strategies earn traders a profit when there is no market movement. Bearish options strategies benefit you when the markets trend downwards, while bullish strategies benefit traders when the markets trend upwards or on the rise.

Option Spreads

All the options mentioned above strategies function properly based on Spreading. Options Spreads can be described as options positions taken in the market. These positions include the functions of buying and selling options contracts all at the same time. The aim of using options Spreads is to come up with distinct profiles with a desirable payoff. These are also known as risk graphs.

All the various options strategies stem from these payoff profiles. Understanding Spreads and how they work, including the different mechanics, makes it easy to understand all the different types of options strategies.

Terminology Used in Advanced Options Trading

As you continue to educate yourself about advanced options trading, there is a need to learn more about the relevant terminology and definitions. Below are some commonly used terms that you should learn about. These terms will help you understand the mechanics of options and how they function. As an investor or trader, you should endeavor to learn more about these terms and definitions.

Spreads: A Spread can be defined as an order placed by a trader to a broker with instructions to purchase or place two options simultaneously. The broker, through your chosen platform, will then implement the instructions and can place the orders.

The term Spreads can also refer to the process of hedging or specifically opening a hedged position. As a trader, if you are bullish on an option, you will purchase a bullish Call Spread option hoping that the option price will go up so that you later sell it for a profit.

Hedging: The term hedging refers to offsetting, either in full or partly, the risks involved when you invest your funds in options and hence hold a position. For instance, you can buy a risky option and then sell another option to minimize the risks, even though it reduces profitability. Hedged positions are also referred to as Spreads.

Derivative: The term derivative refers to instruments such as stocks whose price or value relies on the price of another. It implies that the stock price is derived from another stock's price, share, or Forex. For example, options are derivatives because their value is determined largely by the underlying security value or price.

Cash-settled: When a trader exercises an option, they do not transfer the shares, but instead, the value of the option is transferred in the form of cash from the seller to the owner. Therefore, the option seller will not transfer shares but will instead transfer cash.

Equivalency: This is a concept in options trading where two varied positions may be different because of the price but very similar because of the risk versus reward ratio. When the risk and reward ratio is the same, then the term used to signify this is equivalency.

Inside market: This term refers to the actual bid-ask value for a single Spread or option. It is generally narrower compared to the published price in the market. If you want to trade, you do not need to accept the prices offered and can do better.

NBBO: This term refers to the National Best Bid and Offer. It actually should be a term for beginners, but unfortunately, it is not.

Open interest: Open interest simply implies the total number of option Spreads that are open and active but are yet to expire or be closed by traders in the market.

Settlement risk: This refers basically to the risk of managing a position when you are dependent on the markets' opening price. We can also refer to settlement risk as to the profit lost or gained by agreeing to the settlement price as it is on the 3rd Friday of each month, and not that which is determined on Thursdays as with European style options.

How Options Are Priced

You must understand exactly how options are priced. Generally, the price of options will consist of 2 components. These are the intrinsic and extrinsic values. For instance, we know that the intrinsic price generally relies on the strike price's value based on the underlying stock's value. It is also known as the money-ness of options.

While we understand how the intrinsic value is arrived at, things are not so clear with the extrinsic value. It is often a factor of the markets and includes a measure of the risk taken by traders. So how is this value determined?

Numerous factors come to play when you sell options or buy stocks. These factors play a crucial role in determining the level of risk that you are willing to take. They include the total amount of money needed to secure a position, the expected stock price movement within a given time frame and a lot of others. Experts have been trying to develop a suitable formula to work it out for a long time. This formula is intended to take all these different factors into consideration.

There are a couple of mathematical models in use today that tend to provide reasonable extrinsic value measures. The "Black-Scholes Model" is the one that's best known among these models. This model is considered one of the most reliable formulae and among the best solutions for pricing options. It has helped develop a few more complex formulae that are also widely used.

BSM or Black-Scholes Model focuses on five extremely crucial factors. These five factors are represented on the formula using the Greek alphabet. They are Gamma, which represents the rate of change of sensitivity, Delta, which stands for sensitivity to change of the underlying security's value; Vega, which represents volatility; Theta which measures time decay.

Therefore, by using the Black-Scholes Model, traders can arrive at the theoretical value of stock options. This way, traders will easily compare this outcome with the actual value of options traded at the markets. It makes it possible to determine whether options in the market are under or overpriced.

Reward to Risk Ratio

As a serious options trader, you should first work out the risk to reward ratio before even placing an order. This way, you will easily be able to determine whether a particular trade is worth investing in. You will also be able to determine whether your investment objects can be met through the trades you wish to enter.

Options Expiration Cycles

Some particular stocks and securities have options with different expiration months, whereas other stocks and securities have larger or smaller expiration periods. Some securities even have two sets of options with similar expiration dates. It is basically because stock options are assigned with different expiration cycles. When you have a mix of options with varying expiration cycles, you will end up with different stocks and varying underlying securities, all with differing expiration dates.

Options Greeks

Greeks are commonly used in options trading. The Black-Scholes Model uses five different Greek symbols. These symbols are collectively known to traders as the Greeks or Options Greeks. Even though those within the options trading community question the Black Scholes Model's accuracy, it is widely used and generally accepted as a tool for providing value to stock options. Several popular options trading strategies are popular today are based on this model.

Delta Neutral Trading

Options trading basics have taught traders how to benefit from all types of market conditions, including upward and downward trends. It is through the use of different options strategies for trading purposes. However, it is also possible to develop stock market positions independent of the underlying stock's price movement.

These are generally referred to as Delta neutral positions. Traders generally love Delta neutral positions in the market because they can properly and accurately determine positions that will offset any price movement of the underlying security. Such positions allow traders to benefit from the rise of the implied volatility of underlying security. Traders also benefit from the general time decay of the positions they hold. It means that you can have a 100% winning position, which is really what every trader would love.

Implied Volatility

Two factors affect the price of options more than all others. These are implied volatility and underlying stock's value. What greatly affects an option's extrinsic value is the implied volatility of a security, while the underlying security price affects its intrinsic value. Therefore, as the value of implied volatility increases, so does the option's price, mainly because of an increase in extrinsic value.

Demand also affects implied volatility in a big way. There is always an increase in implied volatility when there is a high demand for a stock or its affiliated options. IV or Implied Volatility opens doors for other profitable ventures as well. One of these is speculation, especially on future volatility. When you buy stock options and the Implied Volatility is low, you will likely earn a decent profit with a rapid increase of Implied Volatility. It is true even when the price of the underlying security does not move.

Another popular method of benefitting from implied volatility is to write stock options at elevated levels of implied volatility, then close these positions when there is a reduction in implied volatility. It just shows how crucial implied volatility is when it comes to options trading, and understanding the concept is necessary.

Understanding Options Leverage

Sometimes traders use options for leverage purposes. In such instances, it is advisable to be able to work out the leverage being used. It is important because traders sometimes over-leverage, and this hurts their trades.

Therefore, learning about options leveraging and applying this knowledge to trades will help avert significant losses that would otherwise occur. It also helps to avert other undesirable surprises and provides traders with sufficient control, especially when it comes to your portfolio's volatility.

Market Makers

Sometimes, options traders never pause to think about who is selling the different options that they buy. However, some do pause and wonder who could be losing all the money that they keep making. Most traders are just glad to be making money and not losing any at the markets.

There is a group of finance and investment specialists who are from some of the large financial institutions. These investors are known as market makers because they are the ones who come to the market with funds. They are the ones you deal with, and the finance professionals keep the options markets liquid. Their presence in the markets ensures that you will always be liquid and will always be able to buy and sell options whenever you choose.

When the market makers enter the market, they place their bids and then purchase all the market available throughout the trading day. It means that there will never be a time when you are unable to purchase or sell options.

Level 2 Quotes

By now, you know that as a trader, you do deal directly with market makers. These finance experts infuse the market with funds and make it liquid. In many instances, options traders would love information on which specific traders to deal with, even directly. It is even in some cases where they stand to make a mere $0.10. It may seem like a tiny amount, but it does add up, and the final figure can be quite impressive.

Level 2 quotes are quotes that traders receive directly from market makers. At level 2, you will receive or view all the different listed quotes provided by individual market makers. If you are an options trader and are a day trader more than anything else, you will likely be successful dealing at level II. These are ideal for options traders looking to make small but significant amounts, trading quickly throughout the day.

Synthetic Options with Options Trade

One of the reasons why traders and investors prefer options trading over other forms of trading is the flexibility that they offer. For instance, you can convert your Call options and Put options without even having to close your hold positions. The ability to alter or transform a short position into a long position and the other way around provides traders with a chance to benefit from different market conditions and volatile and fast-changing market envIronments. It also helps to cut down on commissions that you would otherwise have to pay.

The term synthetic positioning refers to when a trader combines an option position with another or with some stocks to develop different options Spreads.

Options Arbitrage

As you trade options, you can also generate profits in a risk-free manner through options arbitrage. The term options arbitrage refers to when a trader uses special options strategies to benefit from discrepancies in options prices.

The price discrepancies do happen, but they are very rare and occur only occasionally. When they occur, plenty of traders rush in fast to benefit quickly. Options arbitrage provides a reliable source of risk-free profits when trading options.

Options Trading Styles

Trading options at the markets is a versatile method that allows traders to trade in various styles and methodologies. To be a successful options trader, you need to identify and select a trading style that matches your lifestyle and personality. It is critical if you are to succeed as a trader. Should you make blunders and select the wrong style, then your trading exploits will suffer a great deal, and you will not perform as well as you would have, had you selected the correct style.

One of the main reasons why most beginners fail is because they often select the wrong trading styles. Understanding the different trading styles and choosing the right one for you is crucial for successful trading. With the right trading style and proper investment education, you should expect to fair well and be a successful trader for years to come.

Options Legging

As an advanced trader dealing in complex strategies, you will need to learn about legging. It would help if you learned how to leg into a position. Legging is a crucial trading skill that you should master. As a trader trading complex strategies with multiple leggings, you will sometimes need to apply legging techniques for better outcomes.

When you leg into a position, you enable each aspect of your trading strategy to receive attractive pricing, which will increase your profits. In some cases, during options trading, the profit margins may be so minute that legging may be the catalysts to lift profitability to meaningful levels.

Options Assignment

As an options trader, you must understand that the positions you hold in the market regarding your options could easily be assigned before expiration to others. It is true, especially if you are placing Credit Spreads or writing options strategies. Options assignment happens automatically at any time so long as the options have not expired.

CHAPTER 1:

Principal Strategies

Covered Call

A Covered Call corresponds to a financial exchange where an equivalent number of the underlying security is held by an investor selling the Call Options. To do this, the investor is keeping a long position in either an asset sells Call Options to create a revenue stream on the same asset. The investor's long position throughout the investment is "cover," as it means that if the buyer wishes to utilize the Call Option, the seller will deliver the shares. It is described as a "buy-write" trade if the investor purchases the stock simultaneously and sells Call Options against this kind of stock position.

A Covered Call would be a common options technique used in options premiums to generate revenue. Any trader keeping a long position through an asset sells Call Options on the same asset to conduct a Covered Call. Many who wish to retain the underlying asset for such a long time are often optimistic but do not anticipate a substantial price rise shortly. For an investor who thinks the underlying price would not change much through the near-term, this approach is perfect.

With Calls, buying a Naked Call Option is one technique. A basic protected Call or purchase-write may also be structured. It is a widespread tactic because it increases sales and decreases the likelihood that the stock alone will be long. The tradeoff is that even at a fixed price, you must be able to sell your stocks. You buy the underlying asset as you usually might and subsequently write or sell a Call Option on individual shares to implement the strategy.

Naked Call

Only experienced traders should use this strategy. The risk potential in this strategy is unlimited, and the profit potential is also unlimited. That's why this strategy is not fit for beginners and intermediate traders.

In this strategy, you sell a Call option for an asset that you don't own. Due to this fact, this strategy is Called a Naked Call strategy because your position is highly exposed.

For instance, if you have a bullish view of the market and believe that the XYZ stock price will crash, you can sell a Call option for that trade.

You get to pocket the premium obtained for that stock.

If the stock price comes down, you get to keep the premium, which would be your pure profit.

However, if the price of that stocks starts soaring, and that can happen any time, the Call buyer may choose to exercise the right to buy the stocks. In that case, you will have to buy the shares at market price and sell them to the buyer at the strike price. The difference between the prices will be your loss.

The profit potential in this strategy is unlimited as the price of a stock can rise to any level. Although monumental rises normally don't take place in the stock market, there is a probability of that happening in the case of some significant event like a big merger or any other significant news.

If that happens, you will have to buy the stocks at the market price.

Your maximum potential will always remain the premium you can get. But your risk can be huge.

Although this doesn't happen very often, there is a possibility, and that's why this strategy is not suitable for beginners and intermediate traders. It would help if you only adopted this strategy when you have a good understanding and experience of the market.

If they already have a short-term interest in the stocks and an unbiased opinion about its course, investors may opt to use this strategy. They may be trying to generate revenue by selling the Call premium or hedge against a possible decrease in the underlying stock price.

Covered Calls are indeed a balanced strategy, suggesting that the trader only expects a small rise or decline in the corresponding stock price for the term of a written Call contract. This approach is often used when a trader has an unbiased short-term view of an asset and, for this specific purpose, keeps the asset long and has a short position through the option to earn money through the option premium time.

Put, when an investor plans to retain the underlying asset for a long time and therefore does not expect a substantial price rise soon, then while they ride out the downturn, they will generate revenue for their account.

A Covered Call acts as a short-term hedging instrument on something like a long stock position. It enables investors to gain revenue for writing the option through the premium collected. Nevertheless, the lender forfeits stock profits if the price moves beyond the strike price of the option. If the buyer, at any time, wants to exercise the option, they are obliged to provide 100 shares only at the strike price.

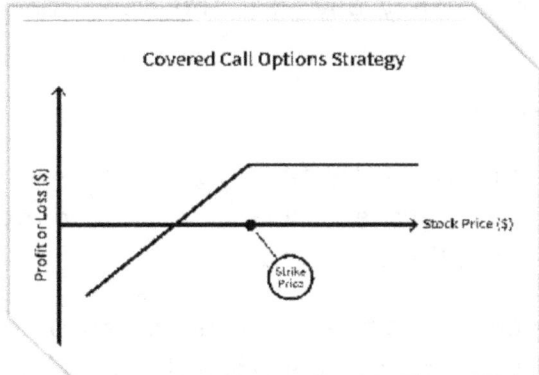

Note in the above profit and loss diagram that the negative Profit and Loss from the Call are balanced by the shares' long position as the stock price rises. Since the investor collects a premium from the Call's sale because as the stock rises upward through the market price, the premium they earn enables them to sell their shares efficiently at a greater level than the market price: the strike price, including the earned premium. The P&L graph of the Covered Call looks remarkably like such a short, naked P&L graph.

For a very optimistic or very pessimistic investor, a Covered Call strategy is not beneficial. They are usually better off not selling the option and only maintaining the stock if an investor is enthusiastic. The option limits the stock profit, decreasing the trade's net profit if the stock price rises. Likewise, if a trader is pessimistic, they would be better off immediately selling the stock. If the stock dives, the premium collected for selling a Call Option will do nothing to cover the stock loss. The Covered Call's gross benefit seems to be the equal of the Short Call Option's strike price, minus the underlying stock's selling price, plus the premium paid. The maximum loss is equal to the underlying stock's selling price minus the premium paid.

The blanketed acquisition strategy means that the operator writes a name alternative on the stock. It is already bought or owned. In addition to incomes at the top rate in the sale, with Calls blanketed, the holder also has gotten entry to the advantages of proudly owning the underlying asset as much as the strike charge. The stocks could be withdrawn.

There are many exclusive applications of the included Call strategy. Some use the approach to make extra profits on the knowledge, which might be feasible while markets are surprisingly stable. It is a great options strategy among traders because, further to the former, investors can take advantage of capital gains if the underlying asset increases in the fee. Money buying (OTM) transactions take place while the outlook is impartial bullish.

When to Use the Covered Call

The Covered Call method is commonly open 30 to 60 days before expiration. It lets an operator profit from the decrease in time. Of route, the top-rated time to put into effect the method relies upon the buyers' targets.

If the aim is to sell Calls and make money on shares, it's first-class if there isn't much difference between the stock rate and the strike charge. If the idea is to promote the stock and the decision, you should be in a function in which the Calls will be assigned. For this to take place, the share rate needs to stay above the strike price to maturity.

Some investors promote stocks and buy stocks in equal time. This approach is called purchase-promote and is used to reduce the base price of newly received shares. With hedging stocks, there is no additional margin requirement in stock while you've got them. When promoting the stock, a suitable premium is 2% of the present-day percentage price (the first foreign money for the stock fee). You need to realize how you could enjoy the approach and set the top rate accordingly. Investors will get hold of a better top class while selling options if the volatility involved is high. For this purpose, many buyers want to keep stocks and then promote Call alternatives at an excessive top class to mitigate the chance of losing a declining stock.

Profit/Loss

The maximum gain with this approach is the difference between the strike fee and the current stock and the Call option settlement sale's primary receipt. Pay interest to the hazards of this method. The capability loss from this method can be substantial.

This loss happens while the fee of the underlying asset falls. However, compared to stock trading, the decline is slightly less painful because of the primary receipt for lowering the stock's downward motion.

Break-even

The break-even point is the distinction between the stock's contemporary price and the primary received from all alternatives' sale.

Example

To recognize OTM Calls, let's consider the following example: A dealer buys 100 shares of stock at $20 in May and writes a June 25 OTM name for $2. If at the expiration of the options, the stock's rate is $28, the strike price of $25 is lower than the stock charger. As a result, the Call is assigned, and the author sells the stocks at $25. Here the dealer would have made $5 at the stock movement, plus $2 at the Calls, for a total income of $7. What if the stock fee had fallen as opposed to increased? In this example, the author will have a loss on the stocks, however again, at the Calls from which they will expire unnecessarily. If the trade becomes trading at $ 17, the dealer might have lost $ 3 within the room, but because he bought Calls for $ 2, his net loss could have been most effective at $ 1.

Married Put or Protective Put Strategy

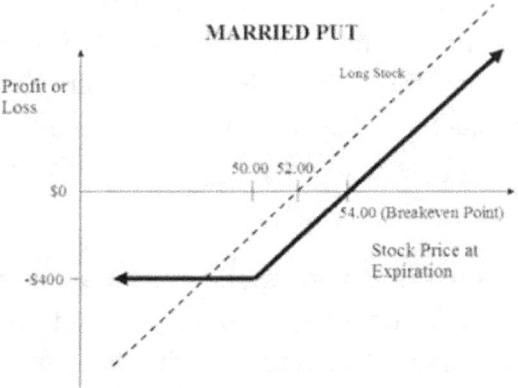

A Married Put is just the term given to the options trading strategy. An investor buys an at-the-money Put Option on the same stock, maintaining a long position throughout a stock, to hedge against devaluation in its price.

The advantage is that even in the worst case, the investor will lose a very small amount of cash on the stocks but still takes part in any profits from price growth. The limitation is that a fee is paid for the Put Option, and it is typically significant. A Married Put can be compared to a Covered Call.

This options strategy safeguards an investor from a dramatic decline in the corresponding stock price. This strategy can be made prohibitive by the expense of the alternative. Based on the movements in the stock, the Put Options differ in price. The strategy could work well for low-volatility assets where traders are anxious about potential news that would dramatically change the price.

Likewise, as an insurance plan for clients, a Married Put works in the same manner. Whenever the investor is worried about possible near-term risks in the stock, it is a constructive technique. The investor also enjoys stock ownership advantages, like collecting dividends and voting rights by holding the stock with such a protective Put Option. On the other hand, though equally as positive as holding stocks, merely owning a Call Option does not confer the same benefits.

Both a Long Call and Married Put have the same infinite profit opportunity, as the underlying stock's price growth does not have a cap. However, profit is still significantly smaller than it will be for just holding stocks, diminished by the cost or premiums of the acquired Put Option. The Break-even point for the strategy is reached when the underlying stock increases by the sum of the premium-charged options. The benefit is something over that number.

Married Put's advantage is that there is a base under the stock that reduces downside risk. The base is the distinction between the value of the commodity stock and the price of the Put only when the married Put was purchased. Alternatively, suppose the underlying stock sold exactly at the strike value at the end of the option acquisition. In that case, the technique's loss is limited to precisely the premium charged for the option.

A married position is also known as a synthetic Long Call, as it has a similar profile of benefit. The method is similar to using a standard Call Option since the same dynamic applies to both: restricted loss and infinite benefit potential. The distinction between these methods is essentially how far lesser capital is needed to purchase a Long Call.

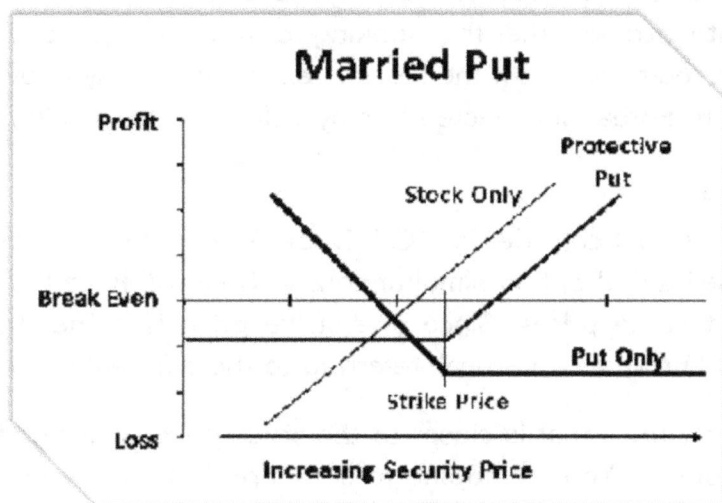

In the Profit and Loss graph shown above, you will see that the losses are reduced as the share price falls with all the long stock and Long Put positions together. Nevertheless, the stock is eligible to partake in the appreciation beyond the premium spent on the Put. The P&L graph of a Married Put looks identical to the P&L graph of a Long Call.

A Married Put arrangement is an investment-preserving tactic rather than just a profit-making technique. Indeed, the value of the aspect of the plan put into place becomes a built-in price. The Put price decreases the plan's viability by the option's expense, implying that the underlying stock rises higher. Consequently, as an insurance contract against short-term volatility in the otherwise favorable stock or as a defense against an unexpected price downturn, traders should be using a Married Put strategy.

Newer investors can benefit from realizing that their stock risks are minimal. It might offer them more optimism as they understand more about various strategies for investing. Of course, this coverage comes with a price tag, which involves the option price, fees, and probably other charges.

Credit Spreads vs. Debit Spreads

The next options strategies that we are going to look at involve unidirectional trading again. The first strategy that we are going to examine is called Debit Spreads. You can form a Debit Spread using either a pair of Calls, which you would use if you are hoping to see the stock rise in price, or a pair of Puts, used when you expect the stock to drop. These essentially serve the same purpose as trading Calls and Puts; however, they provide mitigated risk strategies.

Next, we will look at Credit Spreads. Credit Spreads are a completely different way of trading to generate income rather than looking for the stock to move in a certain way. You can use Put Credit Spreads if the stock is expected to stay above a certain value or use Call credit to Spread if expected to stay below a certain value.

Call Debit Spreads

The first strategy we will consider is a Call Debit Spread. In this case, you will buy a Call option and sell a Call option simultaneously. They will have the same expiration date but different strike prices. Since one strike price is higher than another, the Vertical Spread is known as a Vertical, referring to the different strike prices.

A Call option with a price that is closer to the stock price is worth more money, and you will buy this option. You are hoping to earn a profit from the lower strike price.

You would enter a Call Debit Spread for the same reasons you would buy a Call option—you are expecting the stock price to increase before the options expire. The purpose of the Call with the higher strike price is to mitigate losses. You will sell that Call option.

Selling a Call option with a higher strike price will lower the cost required to enter the position. However, it creates a tradeoff because it will reduce the amount of profit you can make. Like an Iron Condor, a Call Debit Spread is a limited risk and limited reward strategy. The probability of earning a profit is increased, and your total risk is limited. Still, your profits are also capped, unlike with simply trading Call options, which at least in theory have unlimited profit potential.

The maximum profit you can earn on a Call Debit Spread is found by taking the difference between the two strike prices and then subtracting the premium paid to enter the position. Maximum profit is attained with a Call Debit Spread if the stock price rises to or above the higher strike price. The difference between this type of trade and simply buying a Call is that no matter how high the share price rises above the higher strike price, your profit is fixed.

The maximum loss is the net premium paid to enter the position. Let's look at some specific numbers to get a better handle on the Call Debit Spread.

Let's say some stock is trading at $80 a share. We will create a Call Debit Spread by buying a Call option with a strike price of $80 and selling a Call option with a strike price of $84. We will assume that there are 15 days to expiration.

The Call with the $80 strike price is going to cost $123. We sell the Call with the $84 strike price, and that brings us a $16 credit, lowering the cost to enter the position to $107. So, the maximum profit on a per-share basis is:

Difference in strikes – net cost to enter position = $4 - $1.07 = $2.93

Or for 100 shares, our profit will be $293.

The break-even price for a Call Debit Spread is the strike price of the Call we purchase plus the net premium paid. In this case, that would be $80 + $1.07 = $81.07. Profits will gradually increase until we arrive at the $84 strike price, where we get the maximum profit. The maximum profit remains fixed for any higher share price.

Put Debit Spread

If you believe that instead of increasing the stock price will drop, but you want to mitigate the potential losses from investing in Put options, you can invest using a Put Debit Spread. It works similarly to a Call Debit Spread, but with everything adjusted to Put options.

A Put Debit Spread involves simultaneously buying and selling a Put option. We will buy a Put option with a given strike price and then sell a lower strike price option.

The maximum loss that can occur with this trade is the net premium paid, which is the price paid for the higher strike price. Put less the premium received as a credit for selling the lower strike price Put option.

The break-even point is the higher strike price less the net premium paid.

If we have a stock trading at $100 a share and expect the share price to drop, we can buy a Put option with a $100 strike price and sell a Put option with a $95 strike price. A Put option with a $100 strike price will cost $1.25. A Put option with a $95 strike price will net a premium of $0.07, so the total cost to enter the position is $1.18.

The maximum profit is the difference in the strike prices minus the total cost to enter the position, which would be $5 - $1.18 = $3.82.

From these examples, you can see that choosing strike prices that are Spread out increases the maximum profit that can be made but at the expense of reducing the mitigation in risk that selling the second option provides.

Put Credit Spreads

We are going to talk about options trading strategies that are designed to earn income. Income-generating strategies that involve Puts and Calls without using something like an Iron Condor can be Spreads, or they can be traded "naked." In this section, we are going to be looking at selling Put Credit Spreads.

When selling a Put Credit Spread, you don't care what the stock is doing as long as it doesn't drop to the level of your strike prices. And so, you are looking to sell out-of-the-money Put options and then mitigate your risk by purchasing a Put option. It will help limit your losses if the option you sell is exercised and the stock price has also dropped below the second-strike price.

The way to set up a Put Credit Spread is to sell a Put option at a relatively high strike price. However, the strike price should be such that the Put option is out-of-the-money. You don't want to sell an in-the-money Put option—because the Put option will be exercised when this expires, and you'd have to buy the stock. We are setting up this kind of trade, hoping that the option will not be exercised.

It is an income-generating trade, so we will receive a credit to our account for entering the trade. Then after this, we hope that the price moves along such that the options expire worthlessly. So, we will hope that the strike price stays above the strike price used for the Put option that we sell, but other than that, we don't care what the stock does.

The closer the strike price of a Put option is to the stock's market price, the more it will be worth. But that also increases the probability that the option can expire in-the-money, so some care needs to be used. Many successful traders trade Put options that are far outside the money, at least a standard deviation. It significantly reduces the probability that they are going to expire in-the-money. But the downside is that you will make less money per trade, and to make an income, you would need to enter into many trades.

The maximum profit earned on a Put Credit Spread is the net premium you receive for entering the position. It is a sell to open position, and you will receive a net credit given by the premium received for the higher strike price minus the premium paid for, the lower strike price.

The maximum loss on the trade is figured from buying and selling shares when the options are exercised. Maximum loss is going to occur when the share price drops below the lower strike price.

Even though you receive a credit for entering into this position, you have to Put collateral into your account to make the trade. The collateral is enough cash so that you could cover the maximum loss that should occur. Let's look at a couple of real-world examples.

Google is trading at $1,229.93 a share. We can set up a Put Credit Spread by selling a Put option with a strike price of $1,232.50 and buying a Put option with a strike price of $1,222.50. The two Put options used in a Put Credit Spread will have the same expiration dates. Selling a Put option is how you make money on this trade, and you buy the other Put option to limit the maximum possible loss, should the stock price drop unexpectedly.

It is another limited-risk, limited-reward type strategy. This strategy has fixed profits and losses when entering the trade.

In the case of Google, the $1,232.50 Put option is selling at $12.60. So, we sell this and receive the premium. The $1,222.50 Put option is $7.60. We make the profit on this trade is equal to the difference in prices required to enter the trade, $12.60-$7.60 = $5. We would earn $500 from this Spread if the share price were at or above the upper strike price at expiration.

Now let's look at possible losses. Suppose that the share price stays below the upper strike price. The break-even point is the upper strike price minus the premium paid. We are thinking of the buyer's break-even price because we want to see at what point they would exercise that option. With a high price like this, $12.50 to buy the Put option, the break-even price is $1,232.50 - $12.50 = $1,220. So, the stock has to drop to $1,220 before it's even worth exercising the option.

But let's say the share price drops low enough so that we hit maximum losses, as the share price drops below the lower strike price, to say $1,210 a share. In that case, the Put option we sold will be exercised, meaning that we have to buy shares of stock at the higher strike price of $1,232.50. That is a bad scenario for sure, but we can now sell them at the strike price for the other Put option, which we had purchased to mitigate risks.

Therefore, we sell the shares at $1,222.50. So right now, we are at a loss of $10 a share, but we received a net credit of $5 a share. Subtracting this from our loss, the total loss on the trade is limited to $5 a share, or $500 in total.

In many cases, it might be more likely that the option gets exercised. If the share price is between the two strike prices, your losses will be lower than if the share price drops below the lower strike price. The function of the lower strike price is to put a cap on the possible losses.

To enter into the trade, you would have to make sure that there was enough money in your account to cover possible losses. So, in this case, we'd need to have about $500 in our account to act as insurance.

Assuming that you are picking good trades, you will not experience losses most of the time. So, you can use your collateral over and over again when making trades. In this case, you could do weekly repeats of the same trade. Most traders pick around 3-4 stocks that they want to focus on. This approach allows you to get to know the company well, and so you will be able to have an idea of how the stock moves and make good choices for your strike prices. You could then trade Google every single week, selling Put Credit Spreads that expire every Friday. Using this method, you could cobble together a pretty high six-figure income using the collateral of a few thousand dollars.

Call Credit Spreads

There is another approach, which is to use Call Credit Spreads. Under most market conditions, traders prefer to use Put Credit Spreads. But in a bear market, Call Credit Spreads may be more appropriate since, with a Call Credit Spread, you expect the stock to stay the same or drop in value.

With a Call Credit Spread, you will sell a Call option with a lower strike price and buy a Call option with a higher strike price. To be successful, you will sell your Call option that is out-of-the-money, and you are going to hope that the Call option will stay out-of-the-money.

If a stock is trading at $200 a share, we could sell a Call option with a strike price of $202 with 30 days to expiration for $346. Then we could buy a Call option with a strike price of $210 for $114. So, when you have a Call Credit Spread, you sell an option with a lower strike price out-of-the-money, and then you buy a Call option with a higher strike price that is also out-of-the-money.

The profit is fixed and is equal to the net credit received. For a Call option with a lower strike price, you will receive more money than pay for a Call option with a higher strike price.

The Call option that you buy will help you mitigate the risk if the share price rises. Maximum losses will occur if the share price rises above the higher strike price. In that case, you will be assigned and have to sell shares of stock at the lower strike price, but then you can buy share of stock at the higher strike price and then sell them on the market to recoup some of your losses. The maximum loss will be equal to the difference in the strike prices minus the net credit received.

Buying Back to Close

If you sell Put or Call Credit Spreads, buying back to close is always a viable strategy to avoid assignment. You want to wait until it is close to expiration. Most options are not exercised until they expire, so you can buy back to close and avoid assignment either if the trade has gone bad, meaning that the share price moved in a way against the trade, or you're fearful of a dramatic move of the share price on the expiration day. Suppose you are not concerned about the stock price movements and your options are out-of-the-money as expiration day approaches. In that case, you can let the options expire worthlessly, and, you will receive the maximum possible profit on the trade.

Straddles and Strangles

It type of strategy is used when the stock is expected to make a large pricing move, but you don't know how it is going to move. It involves buying a Call and a Put option together in a single trade. A Strangle involves setting an abounding range for the expected stock movement, using different strike prices for the Put and Call option. A lower strike price is used for the Put option, while a higher strike price is used for the Call option. The break-even price is the break-even price for the Call option if the stock rises or the break-even price for the Put option if the stock drops. For example, if the share price was $100, and it was expected to make a big move, you could set up a Strangle with a $105 Call option and a $95 Put option. If the stock prices fail to move either above the Call option strike price or below the Put option strike price, you will lose money on the trade. The maximum possible loss is the cost of buying the options. The strategy is considered neutral because it will make profits if the stock moves up (strongly) or down (strongly). You will invest in this strategy when you expect a large move in the stock, so many traders buy Strangles before an earnings Call. Most earnings Calls result in the stock's big price movements, but you aren't sure which direction it will move before the Call. The strike prices selected for the Call and the Put option will be out-of-the-money. Both options will have the same expiration date.

The maximum profit on the upside is theoretically unlimited, but it will depend on how far the stock price moves above the Call option's strike. If that happens, the Put option expires worthless, and your profit selling the Call option minus the cost of buying the Put option is your net profit. If the stock price drops, the maximum profit will occur in the extremely unlikely case that it dropped to zero, less the Call option cost. If the stock price moves to any level below the Put option's break-even price, you can earn a profit. A Straddle is used for the same purpose, but in this case, we set the strike prices of the Call and Put option to the same value, and both options will have the same expiration date. With a Straddle, you want the stock price to move off the strike price used in either direction.

Strangle

A Strangle is set up using a Call and a Put option to set a bounded stock price range. Unlike the Iron Condor, the goal, in this case, is to earn profits when the stock price moves outside the boundary that we have created, rather than profiting when the stock price stays inside of it. As the graph below indicates, we will earn a profit when the stock prices are outside the two boundaries set by a Call and a Put option. It is less complicated than an Iron Condor because we will buy two options to trade.

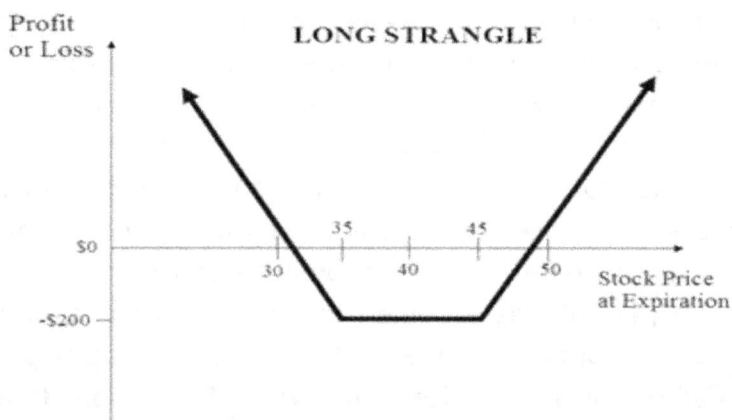

The goal here is to earn a profit from a large change in share price that can move either up or down. You buy a Call option at one strike price, which forms the upper boundary for the trade. Then you buy a Put option at a lower strike price but with the same expiration date that sets up the lower boundary for the trade.

The profit potential for a Strangle is quite large. In theory, the profit potential on the upside is unlimited. Of course, in the real world, stock prices don't increase without a limit. We will look at a specific example to get a handle on potential profits.

So, if the stock price breaks to the upside, the Put option will expire worthlessly. You are out the price paid for the Put option. If the stock breaks to the downside, then the Call option will expire worthlessly.

The setup has two break-even points on each side of the trade. On the upside, the break-even price is the strike price of the Call option plus the total premium paid to buy the two options. On the downside, the break-even point is the strike price of the Put option minus the total premium paid to buy the two options.

So, let's say that we have a stock trading at $200 a share, and we are going to set up a Strangle before an earnings Call. We can buy a Call option with a strike price of $202 for $210. We can buy a Put option with the same expiration date with a strike price of $198 for $205. This way, our total cost is $415 to enter the trade.

The break-even price on the downside is $198 - $2.05 = $195.95. If the stock price drops, it has to drop at least to $195.95 before making a profit. On the upside, the break-even price is $202 + $2.10 = $204.10, and so the stock price has to rise at least to $204.10 before we can start making a profit.

We are assuming that we buy these options 14 days to expiration. Let's say that there is an earnings Call in 7 days so that the price action will take place with six days to expiration. We will assume that the stock price didn't move very much in the interim.

If there are no other changes at six days to expiration, the Put option is now valued at $109, and the Call option is valued at $1.12. So, they have lost quite a bit of value. However, before earnings, Calls implied volatility tends to go up a lot. We will assume that implied volatility spikes to 45% before the earnings Call for our exercise. Under these conditions, the Call option is priced at $370, and the Put option is priced at $364. That gives us a total of $734. They are just based on the volatility we could sell at a profit. Now let's say the earnings Call has some surprises and beats expectations. For a $200 a share stock, a rise in the price of $10, $20, or more is not unusual. Let's say that it rises $20 a share overnight. That causes the Put option to drop to $16 in value, so it is worthless. The Call option spikes to $1,810. We can sell it at a massive profit, found by subtracting the cost of entering the trade:

$1,810 - $415 = $1,395

Now let's say that instead of the earnings, Call has a lot of bad news, and the stock plummets to $170 a share the following morning. In that case, the Put option increases in price to $2,800. This time we make a profit of:

$2,800 - $415 = $2,385

So, we see from this example that we can profit with stock moves in either direction.

What if the stock stays in the range? In that case, we will lose money on the trade. The maximum loss incurred will be the price paid to buy the options. If the share price stays in between the two strike prices, both options will expire worthlessly.

Straddle

Now we will consider a similar trade that is called a Straddle. A Straddle is also designed to earn profits from a breakout to one side or the other. We will buy a Call option and a Put option in the Straddle case, just like we would do with a Strangle. In this case, however, we will have the same strike price for both and the same expiration date. The goal of a Straddle is the same, we hope to profit from large price movements, and it doesn't matter which direction the price goes; up or down is fine. If the price moves to the upside, in theory, the maximum profit is unlimited. In reality, it will be a finite value, minus the total cost required to buy both options to enter the position. Like a Strangle, It is a net debit, and so you buy to open this position. In theory, the stock could lose all of its value to the downside, but of course, that is a very rare event. Either way, you can still make large profits from significant drops in stock prices, such as after an earnings Call. The break-even price is the strike price plus the total premium paid to enter the position to the upside. In this case, the stock price has to rise at least one amount to start earning profits. On the downside, the break-even price is the strike price less the total price paid to enter the position. If the stock price drops, it has to drop at least by this amount before we start earning profits. The maximum possible loss would occur if the share price stayed equal to the strike price used. On a graph of profits and losses, the Straddle forms a V shape, with the bottom representing the maximum loss at the strike price.

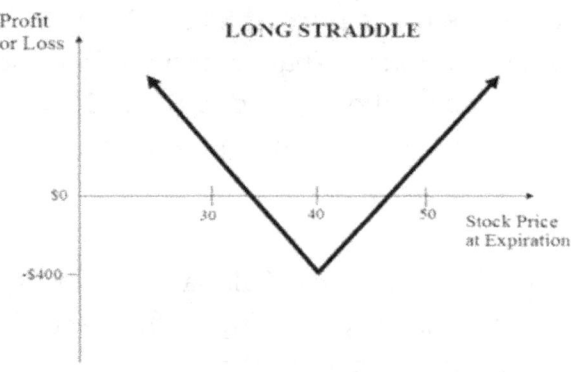

~ 34 ~

Let's say that we are trading Facebook stock at $186 a share. We buy a Call and Put option with the at-the-money $186 strike price with ten days to expiration. With a high level of volatility, say approaching an earnings Call, each option's price would be about $429, so the total cost to enter the position would be $858.

Now say with five days left to expiration, Facebook announces their earnings. If the earnings Call was great news, the stock price could go up, say $15 a share. In that case, the Put option expires worthless, and the Call option rises to $1532 in value, and we earn a profit of:

$1,532-$858 = $674

If the news was bad instead, and the stock dropped $20 a share, the Call option would expire worthlessly, and the Put option would be priced at $2004. Our total profit would be:

$2,004 - $858 = $1,146

Iron Condors

An Iron Condor is one of the most popular options strategies. It is an income-producing strategy, and an Iron Condor is sold for a net credit (keep this in mind, there is a lot of misinformation about Iron Condors). An Iron Condor is sold using a Call Credit Spread and a Put Credit Spread, all in the same trade. The two options with inner strike prices will be sold. So, for example, suppose that a stock is trading at $200 a share. You could sell a Call option with a strike price of $205 and buy a Call option with a strike price of $210. Simultaneously, you would sell a Put option with a $195 strike price and buy a Put option with a $190 strike price. As long as the stock price stays in between the inner strike prices—ranging between $195 and $205 in our example—you will make a profit. An Iron Condor is used when you expect the stock price will not change much over the options' lifetime. All options used in an Iron Condor have the same expiration date.

To pick your strike prices, determine where support and resistance are. You want to set the strike price of the Put option you sell slightly above the support price and set the Call option's strike price a little bit below the resistance price. Then set the outer strike prices slightly above the resistance price level for the purchased Call option and below the support price level for the purchased Put option. Many traders make a full-time living strictly selling Iron Condors. The chart has the following form.

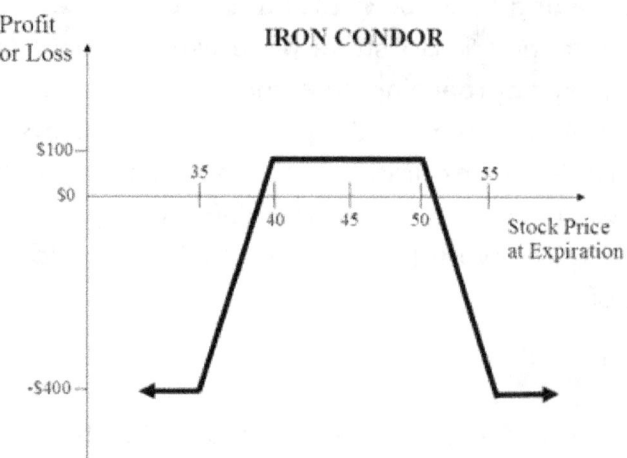

You will receive a net credit for the Call Credit Spread and a net credit for the Put Credit Spread. The total credit received is your maximum profit. If the stock remains in between the inner strike prices, this is when you will earn profits. One advantage of the Iron Condor is that losses are also capped. Should the stock move to the upside, the maximum loss is the difference in the two Call options' strike prices. Should the stock move downward, the maximum loss is the difference between the Put options' strike prices. Using our example here would be a $5 loss (per share – total $500) if the stock moved below $190 or above $210.

The Logic Behind the Iron Condor

The Iron Condor combines a Put Credit Spread and a Call Credit Spread into a single trade. I know, it sounds extremely complicated. Now we are talking about four options in a single trade. But the truth is that it's not that complicated.

So, to set this up, you estimate what the range of the stock is. So you want to look over a reasonable time and then determine what the lowest share price the stock is going to hit will be. It doesn't predict what will happen in the future, but it does give us a boundary point that we can use. It is all about playing the probability game. So we are estimating the probability that the stock is going to stay within some range of values.

Now we do the same for the upper bound. If a stock price doesn't change very much, it will be ranging between these two values without having any breakout.

It is the secret of the success of the Iron Condor. The first step to set it up is to sell a Call option at a higher boundary price. Then, we sell a Put option at the lower boundary price.

Selling these two options gives us a net credit.

The Iron Condor is another limited risk strategy, though. To minimize the risk, we are going to buy two options that lie on the outside range. You will buy a Put option with a lower strike price than the Put option that we sold. You can see now that we have set up a Put Credit Spread.

Next, we buy a Call option with a higher strike price than the Call option that we sold. So, It sets up a Call Credit Spread.

But when you combine the two into a single trade, you set up an interior boundary for the stock to move around in.

Suppose that a stock is trading at $100 a share. We could sell a Call option with a strike price of $105. Then we could sell a Put option with a strike price of $95. It sets up our zone of profitability. As long as the stock stays within the range of $95 to $105 per share until option expiration, we are in a good situation. To mitigate the risk, we buy two options with outside strike prices. So we could go with a Call option with a strike price of $110 and then buy a Put option with a strike price of $90.

The strategy on these is to wait and hope the stock price doesn't break. If it doesn't, you can let the options expire, and you will earn a profit from the net credit you have received. The net credit is going to be given like this:

Credit received selling high strike Put + credit received selling low strike Call − debit paid for high strike price Call − debit paid for low strike price Put.

There is some argument about whether or not you buy or sell an Iron Condor, but people arguing about this are confused. You are selling an Iron Condor. It is because you are selling to open, and you receive a net credit for the trade.

If things go bad, if the stock does have a breakout one way or another, you will have losses, but they will be capped. If it's not working out, you can always buy back the Iron Condor to close the position. As with other trades, if you are risk-averse and worried about something amazing happening with the stock on expiration day, you can always buy back the Iron Condor to close the position early. However, remember that this move will cut down on your profits, which are limited already by the credit received for entering the position.

When to Use An Iron Condor

You want to use an Iron Condor when a stock is not expected to move very much. Some people pick options with very low Delta values like 0.16, so they are far outside the money. It can give the stock a wider range of values to oscillate around it, but you will make smaller profits per option contract. That said, it increases the probability of earning a profit. So once again, we have a tradeoff.

You will not want to Put an Iron Condor on when the stock has a high amount of implied volatility. High implied volatility will mean that there is a higher probability that the stock will move outside one of the boundaries that you have setup with the Iron Condor.

One situation that definitely would not be used with an Iron Condor is before an earnings Call. You do not want to have an Iron Condor on the stock before the earnings Call. If the stock rises to a new range, it might be possible to use an Iron Condor to earn income off the stock after settling down.

You might choose low volatility stocks for Iron Condors. For example, a relatively stable stock like IBM (outside of earnings season) could be a possible choice. But like any options trade, you will want to see what the open interest is on the options you are considering for your Iron Condor.

Why Use an Iron Condor

Traders use Iron Condors because it's a limited risk strategy that can be used to generate regular income from trading. Selling an Iron Condor is analogous to selling a Put Credit Spread in that you are going to need a certain amount of collateral to cover the trade. So, while the Iron Condor is in your account, the money you use to cover it will be tied up until you either close the position or you let the options expire, assuming that you don't incur losses because the share price remains in the range that you've set up for the trade. Let's consider a real-world example. It will show that unlike the Spreads, an Iron Condor has losses on the upside and the downside, with a range of profitability in between. The losses are not necessarily equal. In this example, we consider an Iron Condor on Facebook with strike prices of $192.50 and $212.50. It is quite a wide range; it's wide enough that it might survive the upcoming earnings Call. Maximum losses occur when the share price goes above the high strike price Call or below the low strike price Put. In this example, the high strike price Call is $215.

The low strike price Put is $187.50. To the upside, if the share price rises above $215, there is a maximum loss of $55. On the downside, if the share price goes below $187.50, the maximum loss is $305. The collateral required is always the larger of the two potential losses, so to enter into this trade, you'd have to deposit $305 into your account.

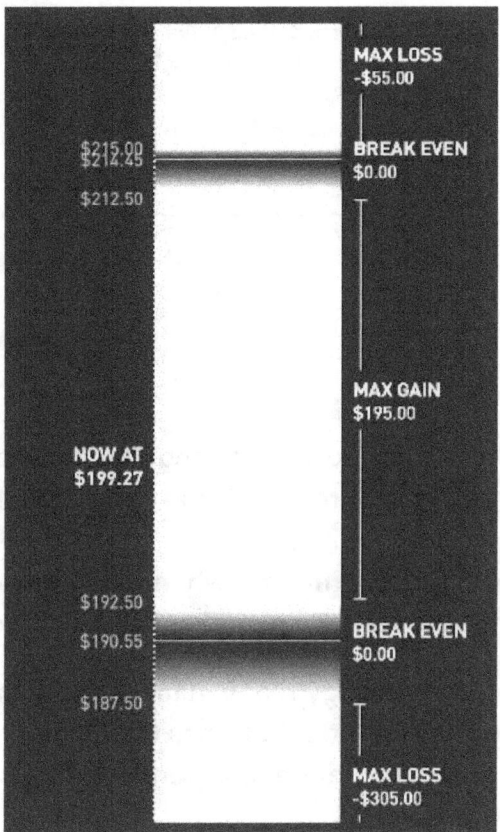

You can see that if the share price stays in between the inner strike prices, the maximum profit of $195 (the credit received for selling to open the position) is realized. The assignment's risk is the same as for a Put Credit Spread or Call Credit Spread—it's not something you have to worry about. If an assignment occurs, the broker is all handled automatically, and the stocks will be quickly bought and sold without you even noticing.

So, the credit received on a per-share basis is $1.95. The upper Put strike price gives the break-even point on the downside minus the credit received, $192.50 - $1.95 = $190.55. The lower Call strike price gives the upper break-even point plus the credit received, so in this case, that would be $212.50 + $1.95 = $214.45.

For the strike prices, you choose out-of-the-money values. An Iron Condor is considered a non-directional strategy. You only care that the share price stays within a given range of values—you don't care if it goes up or goes down within that range.

Butterfly Spreads

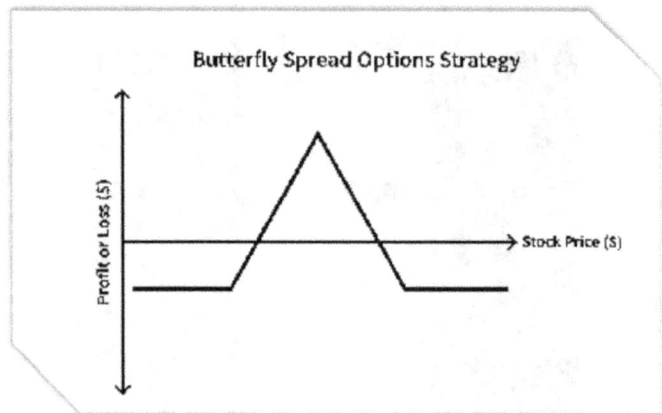

When a stock has a clearly defined positive or negative outlook in the market, the best approaches are Credit and Debit Spreads. But in the case where an underlying asset displays a neural outlook in the market, the best strategy to capitalize on the market is Butterfly Spreads. A stock trend is neutral when it makes no sideways movement or dominant trend to determine an asset's negative or positive outlook.

Butterfly Spreads give you the strategy that is a mix of Bull and Bear Spreads. It draws in four different kinds of options contract but has the same period of expiration. These different contracts will form a price range to determine losses and profits for the trade using three different strike prices.

The upper and middle strike prices must have a distance equal to the middle and lower strike price's distance. At the mid-point strike price, the options trader would have to sell two contracts. At the upper and lower strike prices, the options trader buys two contracts. Butterfly Spreads use both Call options and Put options to reduce the risk level within the specified period.

Therefore, the trader's losses are limited to the initial investment and maximum profits captured when the asset price trades near the mid-point. Therefore, it is very important to consider the condition of neural market analysis before using the Butterfly Spread to mitigate risk while maximizing profitability on the options.

Equity Collar

This strategy is used to hedge risk. It is used on a long stock position that you have, and large traders use this. So, to use this strategy, you would have a large number of shares of some stock. If you are uncertain about the stock's direction that you own, you could set up an Equity Collar to hedge your risk with Put and Call options. You set it up by buying an equal number of Put and Call options with strike prices above the share price for the Call options and strike prices below the share price for Put options. The options will all have the same expiration date. If the share price moves above the Call strike price, you will earn profits on the Call options, and the Put options will expire worthlessly. If the stock price moves below the Put options, the Call options will expire worthlessly. You can exercise the Put options and sell your stock at a higher price than the market price or sell the Put options for a profit and keep your stock.

Short Gut

A Short Gut is a less popular options strategy that involves selling a Call and a Put option simultaneously. You sell the two options with the same expiration month but not necessarily the same expiration date. First, you sell a Call option at a certain strike price, and then you sell a Put option with a higher strike price. Maximum losses are uncapped if the stock price moves in either direction, so you hope the stock price will stay the same. Maximum profit is equal to the premiums received from selling the options. This strategy is little-used, and you must be a level 4 options trader to use it, and you must have enough cash in your account to cover selling the two options (cash as collateral).

Long Gut

A Long Gut involves buying a Call option and buying a Put option with a higher strike price. In this case, you are hoping to profit from the stock moving in either direction, so it is somehow analogous to a Strangle, but you are doing it with the Call's strike prices and Put reversed.

If the stock price moves up, you will make money from the Call but lose money on the Put; if the strike price moves down, viceversa.

Synthetic Strategies

Synthetic strategies are obscure and rarely used by small traders. To make a synthetic Put, you must have a large margin account. To set it up, you will short the stock, so you will borrow shares of stock from the broker and sell them on the market, hoping to buy them back at a lower price. Then you will buy a Call option in the same stock. If the stock price rises, you will make a profit on the Call option to help offset the loss of having to buy the shares back at a higher price (if you borrow shares from the broker, you have to buy them back and return them to the broker at some point). If the stock price drops as expected, you will lose money on the Call option, which will expire worthlessly, but you will make the expected profit from shorting the stock. You can buy it back at the lower share price, return the shares to the broker, and then the profit from doing that minus the cost of the Call option is your net profit. So, this involves shorting stock using a Call option as insurance.

CHAPTER 2:

Advanced Strategies

Long Call

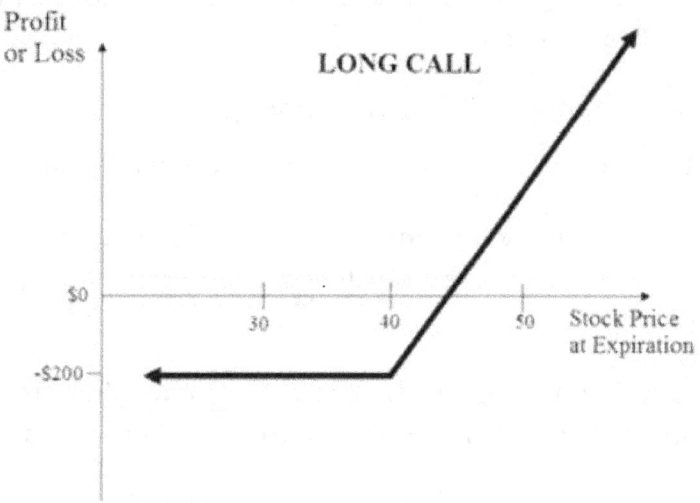

Options terminologies can seem confusing, but you will be good to go once you understand the basics: Long means to buy and Short means to sell. A Long Call option gives you the right to buy an underlying stock at strike price A. It offers you the opportunity to get your game right without getting wiped out directly if you were trading directly in the stock market.

If you feel bullish about a stock (meaning that you hope that a specific stock will rise in value at a point in the future), you can choose to buy the stock outright or use a Long Call option. You will profit in a Long Call option when the stock rises, according to your prediction. But if the opposite happens, you will only lose your premium paid.

Apart from that, Long Calls are less expensive as compared with buying the stock outright. If you were investing in the stock market, a failure for a stock to rise could get you disappointed. You will encounter a lot of risks since you have already bought part ownership into the company.

Suppose you consider entering the market through a bullish strategy. In that case, you need to ensure you thoroughly analyze the time horizon a chosen stock moves in a specific direction and the number of points required for that stock price movement. To minimize risks, what most people do is buy more short-term out-of-the-money Calls. It can be dangerous if all those Calls have not moved successfully to indicate a gain.

The first place to enter the market is through Long Call options. Most beginner options traders enter the market through this area due to its simplicity. It might sometimes be challenging to profit through Long Calls, but it is still not complicated like the advanced option trading strategies.

Risk/Reward Analysis for Long Call Options Strategy

The following entails the risks and rewards to have in mind while using this strategy:

- It involves a little money, making it attractive for beginner options traders. It helps traders to manage their portfolios and avoid trading in stocks that are expensive to buy.

- The loss made is only limited, that is if the underlying stock falls instead of rising. It helps to risk a little money than to lose all in an underlying stock trade.

- There is no need for any complex calculations before executing the stock options plan.

- It does not involve margin debt, and it also has lower commissions than other complex option trading strategies.

- Avoid using all your money in a Long Call option. Buying many out-of-the-money Call options because it is cheap can make you lose your trading capital.

- You need to understand that the Call option is subject to time decay, which depreciates with passing the time towards expiration.

Simple Calculations for Long Call Options

To minimize your losses and maximize your gains, you need to do a simple calculation to overview how the entire Long Call options work. A break-even point is to realize if the underlying financial instrument has neither made a loss or again. The following example will help you understand this better.

Source: Schwab Center for Financial Research (Strategy at Expiration)

>   Long 1 GYZ June 50 Call @ $ 4
>
>   Maximum Loss =$ 400.00 (4.00 option premium paid x 100 shares per contract)
>
>   Break-even Point =$ 54 (4 option premium + 50 strike price)
>
>   Maximum Gain = Unlimited

To calculate the profit potential before aspiration: Profit = [(Rise in underlying stock) x Delta value] / price of Call options

The problem with a Long Call option is that it has a limited life span. Therefore, the underlying stock must move upward very fast above the break-even point to generate unlimited gains for the owner. The downside is that the options' owner stands to lose premium when the underlying stock hasn't moved upward as expected.

Long Put

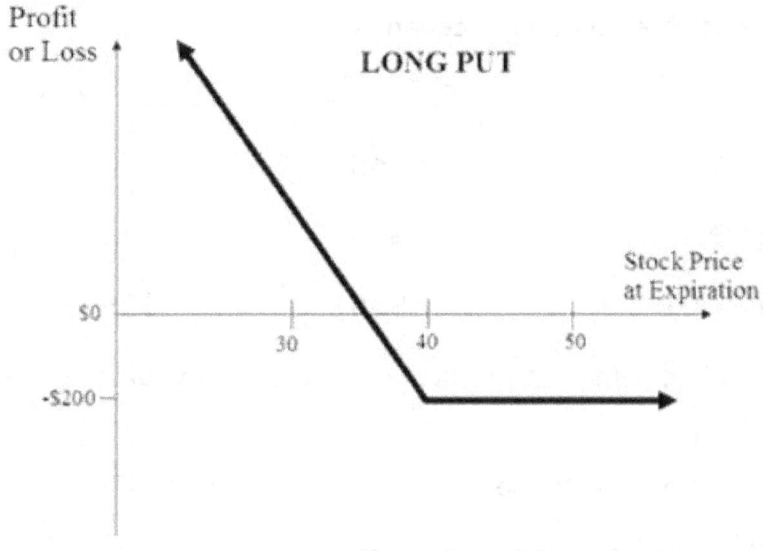

This strategy is also similar to the Long Call strategy. The only difference would be in your outlook on the market. If you have a strong bearish outlook of the stock, you can use the Long Put options strategy.

Even in the Long Put strategy, your profit can be unlimited. The farther down the stock price goes from the strike price, the greater your profit would be.

Unfortunately, if the stock price is trading above the strike price even on the day of the expiry, then your options contract would become worthless.

However, even in a Long Put strategy, your risk is limited to the premium price. No matter how high the stock remains above the strike price, you will have no obligation to pay anything more.

In a Long Put strategy, you are buying the right to sell the stocks at a price fixed now while the current trading price of that stock would be much lower.

For instance, let us again take the fictional stock Gabzo.

It is currently trading at $50.

The expiry is 26 days from now.

You will have several options to choose from.

We will be analyzing three different scenarios:

Moneyness	Strike Price	Current Price	Premium
In-the-money (ITM)	$45	$35	$8
At-the-money (ATM)	$40	$35	$5
Out-of-the-money (OTM)	$38	$35	$2

Let us suppose that your market prediction is right, and your stock price goes down to $35.

Strike price - Current price = Value.

One lot is of 100 shares, and hence your profit would be X100

Your profit in the ITM would be $1 X 100 = $300

Your profit in the ATM would be $11-$5= $6 X 100 = $600

Your profit in the OTM would be $11-$2= $9 X 100 = $900

Like the Long Call strategy, the highest profit would be in the OTM trades, even in the Put options. However, beginners should avoid taking OTM Puts as they are highly risky, and their chances of reaching the target are very low. Therefore, you are more likely to lose all your money on such trades.

Going for the ITM or ATM trades early in the month is usually better for the new traders.

Fig Leaf

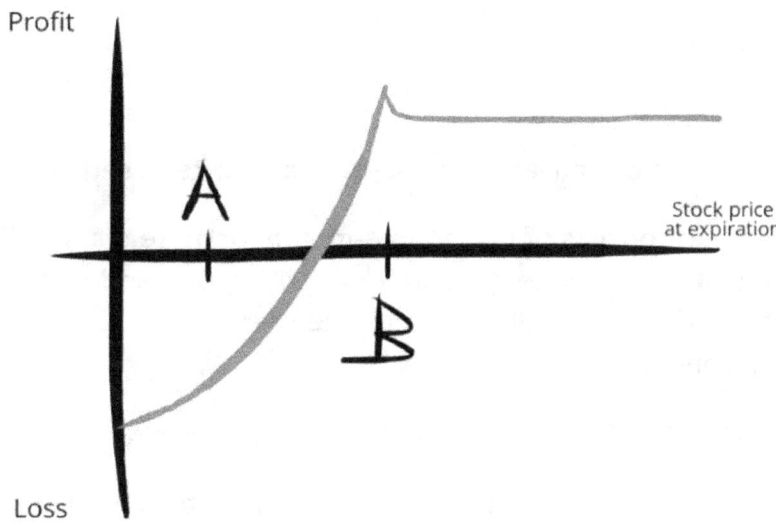

Fig Leaf in Options Trading is similar to its literal meaning in that it is something one should hide behind from the enemy. It is used to mask a short position.

In this case, it is a Long option position used to mask the writer who is Short in the stock or Long in a Call.

The strategy is to hedge the overall risk on the trade. It is an adjustment rather than a strategy as it is designed to reduce risk or leverage.

Long Call Spread

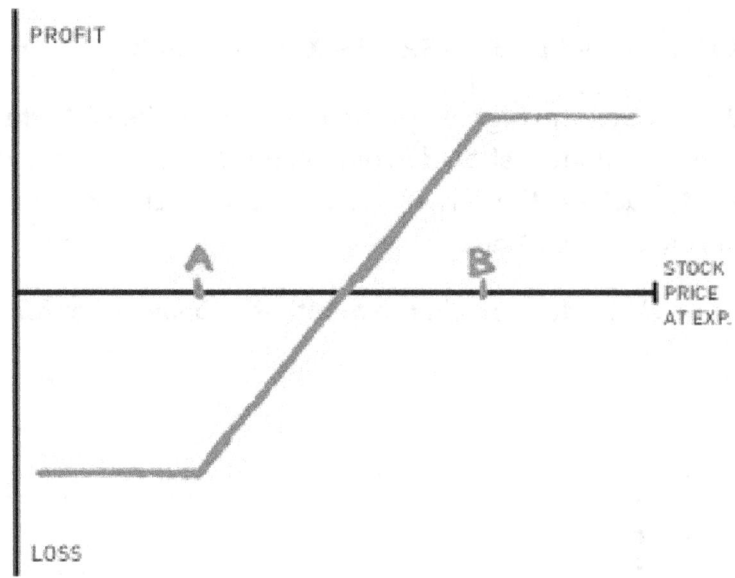

Long Call Spread is a more advanced strategy that is often used as a covering trade.

The Long Call Spread consists of buying one-month (or more distant) Call options with a strike price equal to the underlying stock's strike price and selling an out-of-the-money Call option. The Long Call Spread is often referred to as a Butterfly Spread or double Butterfly Spread.

When executed correctly, the Long Call Spread will provide the following benefits:

1. It offsets the risk of ownership of the underlying stock for a small premium paid for both options.
2. It gives an income stream from both options (long and short) at expiration and until one is exercised, which means that it has unlimited time decay risk.
3. It increases the odds of achieving a profit from a stock move.
4. The price of both options is highly correlated, and therefore the position is usually "covered."
5. The trade can be exited with a minimal capital loss.
6. It can be done on any strike price range, although the Long Call Spread is most frequently used in stocks with relatively narrow price ranges (for example, stocks with a range of only $0.50 to $1.00).
7. It may provide an incentive to buy and hold the underlying stock as it increases in value - especially if selling Puts were part of the strategy.

Long Put Spread

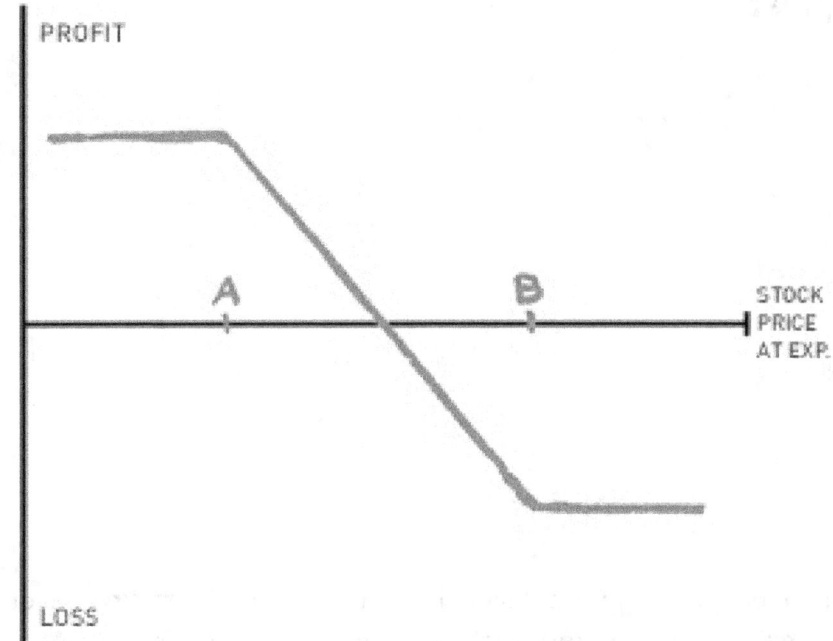

Long Put Spread s are often used in conjunction with short stock positions.

The Long Put Spread consists of buying one-month (or more distant) Put options with a strike price equal to the underlying stock's strike price and selling an out-of-the-money Put option. Like the Long Call Spread, when executed correctly, the Long Put Spread will provide the following benefits:

1. It offsets the risk of ownership of the underlying stock for a small premium paid for both options.
2. It may provide an incentive to buy and hold the underlying stock as it increases in value - especially if buying Calls was part of the strategy.
3. The price of both options is highly correlated, and therefore the position is usually "covered."
4. The trade can be exited with a minimal capital loss.
5. It can be done on any strike price range, although the Long Put Spread is most frequently used in stocks with relatively narrow price ranges (for example, stocks with a range of only $0.50 to $1.00).
6. It may provide an incentive to buy and hold the underlying stock as it increases in value - especially if selling Puts was part of the strategy.
7. It increases the odds of achieving a profit from a stock move.

Short Call Spread

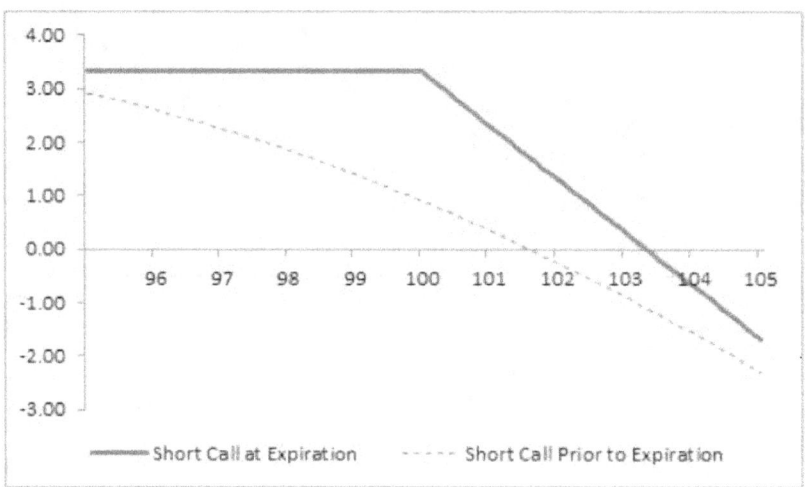

It is a generally clear strategy; however, it requires a high trading level, which isn't generally reasonable for tenderfoots. A Credit Spread is made utilizing two transactions.

It is another directional strategy used by a trader when they believe that their underlying stock has reached its upper resistance level. They do not believe that the underlying stock will go up much more at this point. They usually believe that the stock's price point will stay flat and not change or go back down. It will be the opposite strategy that we talked about earlier with the Bull Put Spread.

Like the Bull Put Spread, the Bear Call Spread is also a Credit Spread. It means that the premium you end up receiving while selling one leg of this trade will be greater than any premium that you end up paying for the second leg of the trade. You will end up receiving a net credit to your account when you decide to go with this position.

The first step in creating your Bear Call Spread is to select the right stock that fits this kind of strategy. You will find various stocks that you can choose from, but you will need to pick based on your outlook for this kind of index.

Next, you will need to sell an OTM Call option of the stock that you selected. And third, you should purchase an OTM Call option with the same expiry date and the same underlying stock as your id with your ATM Call option, but the second one needs to have a higher strike price.

Once you enter the market, you will want to monitor your position each day constantly. Once you have made a considerable profit, which is about 50% of your max profit, it is time to exit your position. Once you have started to recognize some of the market signs and are sure that the stock won't end up reversing, you could wait until the stock reaches its expiry and then takes the maximum profit.

Sometimes, spans are crowned as better for entering a Bear Call Spread than others. You would want to choose the Bear Call Spread any time that you believe that your chosen stock is not likely to rise in price shortly and that this stock is probably going to decline from its current price rather than go up. It can happen when the stock from a particular company that had big market expectations posted their results, and these were way below the expectations of the market. Also, the index option could hit a high resistance level, and this could cause it to go down a bit.

This method won't work that well if the stock is volatile, and it has the potential to rise quite a bit over the short term. You want to pick out some options that are not likely to go up anymore. You would then use the Bear Call Spread and profit whether the stock stays stagnant or the price goes down.

The maximum profit that you will make with the Bear Call Spread is when expiry; the stock price is trading below the strike price of the Call option that was sold. To get the maximum profit, you will need to take the premium received or sell the lower-strike Call option minus the premium paid for purchasing the higher-strike Call option. Then you can multiply both of these by the lot size.

The biggest loss that you would incur with this kind of Spread is when the stock price is trading above the strike price Call option you bought with the higher strike price at the time of expiry. It is why you want to make sure that you are picking out stocks that will go down or remain steady. If the stock goes up with this option, you will end up losing money in the process. It is a good strategy to choose if you think that the market is about to go down or work with a not increasing stock.

The biggest advantage of working with the Bear Call Spread is that it will ensure that the time decay will work in your favor. As long as you go with a stock that can stay below your lower strike price when the expiry happens, you will get the benefit of keeping your entire credit that you received when you entered into this position, and you have the potential to make a good profit.

However, there is a disadvantage of working with this strategy. Suppose you see that there is the possibility that the stock will make a big movement that goes against your expectations. In that case, the maximum amount you could lose can be a lot more than the maximum profit you might have gained with this strategy, so there is some risk.

Short Put Spread

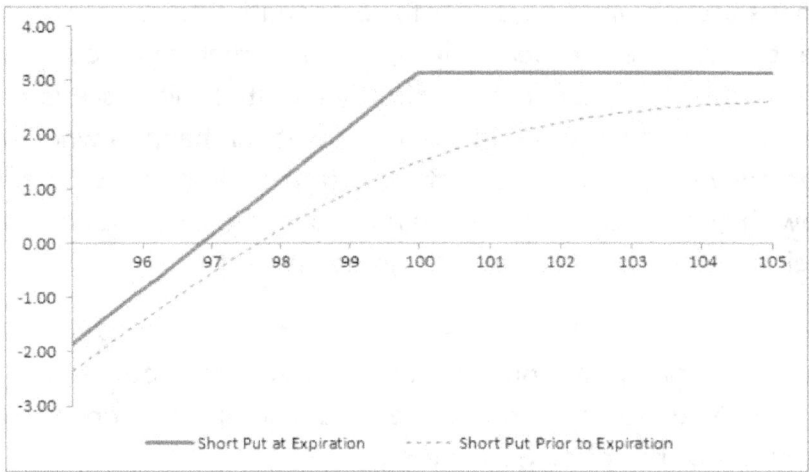

A trader who writes a Put option is referred to as the seller. In this case, an options trader will be required to buy the underlying stock and make sure everything is ready when the buyer is ready to exercise the option. A Short Put option is often referred to as naked or Uncovered Put since the seller is under obligation to purchase shares of the underlying stock before the buyer decides to exercise the right to the option.

Losses can be faced when the Short Put expires worthless without the underlying asset rising above the Put option's strike price. A Short Put should be used if you think underlying security will rise in price more than the strike price determined in the options contract.

To profit in options trading through a Short Put strategy, you need to ensure that the technical analysis conducted leads to a rise in stock price. When the stock price goes down in value throughout the option, the option buyer can choose to exercise the right and hence make you incur potential losses.

However, you will make money through the premiums paid at the signing of the Put options contract. Apart from making money through premiums by opening a Put option, you can also sell a stock at the financial market's underlying price.

For example, say that a stock is currently selling at $ 100 in the financial market. You wish to buy the stock at $ 75. If you consider selling a Put option at a strike price of $ 75 and receive a premium, let's say $ 2.00. If the price of the underlying stock drops to $ 75 as forecasted, then you will get to keep the premium while at the same time buying the underlying stock at the strike price.

Naked Put should be one of the riskiest strategies. Thus, only professionals are best advised to use it. But when that happens, selling Naked Puts can be even safer and more profitable than buying stocks.

When you sell a nude set, you assume that you must buy the stock at a specific price on or before a certain date. You'll knock the price forward for that.

Sales Puts can be a good strategy if you don't come overboard. So, if you're selling nude stocks for $50,000, make sure you buy shares for $50,000, as you may need to continue.

If you do so with moderation, selling Naked Puts has the following benefits:

1. Stocks don't have to go up

When you sell Naked Put shares, you don't necessarily need them to be profitable. You don't have to drop stocks below your bet price.

It will allow you to make money if you have trouble finding stocks that are moving. Instead of taking care of it, you can always sell sets.

2. You can get paid to buy a stock

If the shares fall below the exercise price, you must buy them. But because you got the bonus in advance, it means you got paid to get into a healthy stock, which is much better than buying and maintaining an old way.

And if the company has good long-term growth, you can wait for the weather to rise and sell Covered Calls to get an even higher premium.

3. A premium has been added.

The premium collection eventually adds up and can be very profitable in the long run. You can often earn more by selling sets, and you can do so by maintaining stock.

Is Selling Naked Puts Risky?

Selling Puts can be a great way to make money and get into stocks, but getting away can damage your strategy.

Let's look at two different examples of selling naked sets. In example 1, Mike has $3,000. He wants to invest in an ETF or substantial capital, and he found a fundamentally strong stock that traded at $33. He can now buy and hold 90 shares of that stock or sell $30 well.

Mike decides to go for the second option and sell $30 well. From now on, he earns $150 in advance and is required to buy shares for $30 if the shares rise to $30 or less. From here, one of two things can happen.

1. Shares will drop below $30. He buys it for $30, which is less than what we had to pay for. Mike also has a $150 price he can make up and can keep stocks for a long time

2. Shares remain above $30. Sold expires worthless and runs away $150. Mike may also decide to sell another set next month because he has free capital.

In this case, the sale of the well is not bad. Selling a well can be even safer than buying stocks directly because we make money upfront, which reduces our costs.

In the second example, Fred also invests $3,000. He decided to start selling substantial shares.

He sells one share on XYZ, one on ZTF, and one on ABC, from which he earns $400 but must buy $10,000 if everything turns against him.

In this example, Fred sells high-risk naked sets. Any shares you sell for a bare placement must be held for a long time, and you must be able to buy those shares if you need them.

If all the shares went to Fred, he would have to buy them for $10,000. However, because he does not have $10,000 in his account, he will have to obtain a refund, potentially reducing his account to $0.

In short, one should deal with the sale of Naked Puts from more investment and not from a commercial point of view. If you are not willing to buy and maintain security, you should not sell it naked.

Selling Naked Puts is an excellent choice for a low-risk profit strategy. It is a powerful weapon for any trader because it allows the investor to buy the preferred stock at a price that suits him and gets another price discount. It is a simple strategy that does not require you to look at your computer screen daily and does not require technical analysis hours.

How Do Naked Puts Work?

For example, if XYZ shares trade for $45, the trader may sell the Put for $40 before the next maturity date (i.e., no longer than 30 days). It means that if the stock drops to $40 before the end of the sale, the trader will have to buy 100 shares for $40, which will be $4,000. If the Put's cost were $1.00, the trader would achieve an initial income of $100.

If Put is redeemed and now has to buy shares, his net price would be ($40 - $1 = $39) or $3,900. If the stock doesn't drop to $40 before expiration, Put will fail worthless; the trader keeps $100, and he may sell another set next month, which allows for another discount if his Put is ever applied. Theoretically, traders could keep it indefinitely and eventually buy stocks for nothing! He still has a nice monthly income to make a simple transaction if he never buys shares.

When Should I Sell A Naked Put?

Don't forget to choose the event you want to own. You looked at the basics and decided that even as stocks dwindle, the long-term outlook is good.

Perform a simple analysis of general market trends (S&P, Nasdaq, or DOW) and your share sector groups (the easiest is to see this group's index). Never sell Naked Puts at an apartment or a growing market. NEVER sell in a steady downward trend. If the exchange or sector has a slight downward trend, make sure you have a good idea of the areas of support and how strong they are. It will tell you where to place your Put.

Use the options calculator (like the one available for free at OptionVue Research) and select Put in the range where the stock price is likely to end above the highest target of 80% or better.

Sell Puts before the next month's due date—not further.

Wait for the Put to expire or be executed. If it expires, do it again the following month!

What Else Do I Need to Know?

Even though Naked Put is safer and more advantageous than stock trading, options brokers consider selling Naked Put a risky strategy. Your broker would like to know that you have enough money to buy the selected shares if your Put is exercised. The formula varies between brokers, but a margin requirement is usually required—12% of the stock's full purchase price if you have exercised it.

Why this steep margin requirement? Theoretically, if you buy a stock at Put's best price, it is sometimes because it collapses and may continue to fall until the stock is worthless, leaving you in the dark with the stock you paid too much for. However, if you do not play and do not make an informed decision and choice of your share, this will never happen.

Before sharing the final details, here is a graphical representation of the Naked Put strategy:

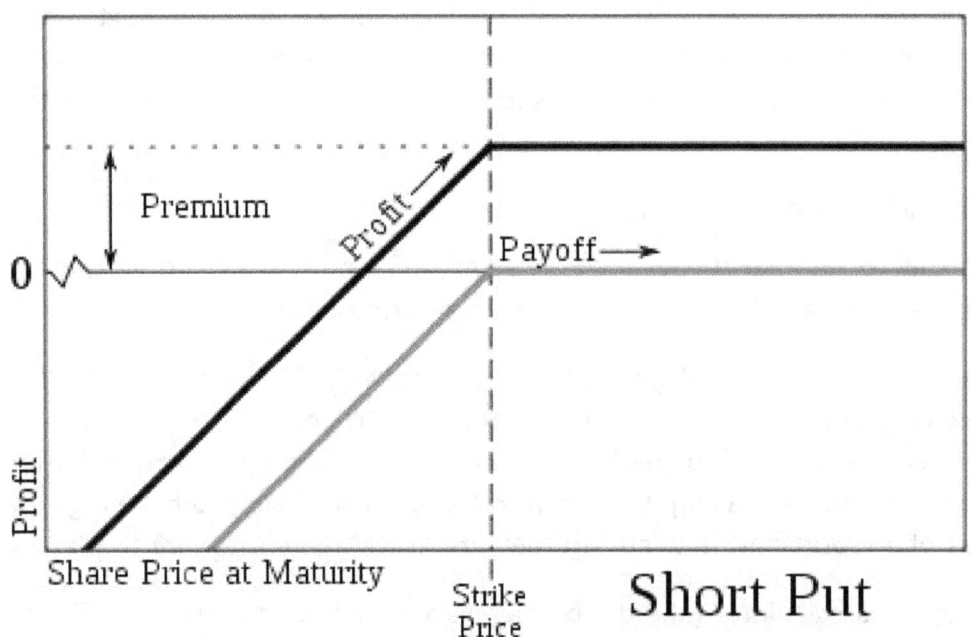

Selling Naked Puts is the only sensible way to buy stocks because you are purchasing those stocks at a discount (why pay more?). In any case, if you usually invest in stocks, you have enough money to meet your margin requirements. In a neutral or bull market, this is a great way to generate a monthly income. It's safe, reliable, and cost-effective, and best of all, it doesn't require a thorough knowledge of technical analysis. Knowing the basics, performing simple trend analysis makes trading is secure.

Long Straddle

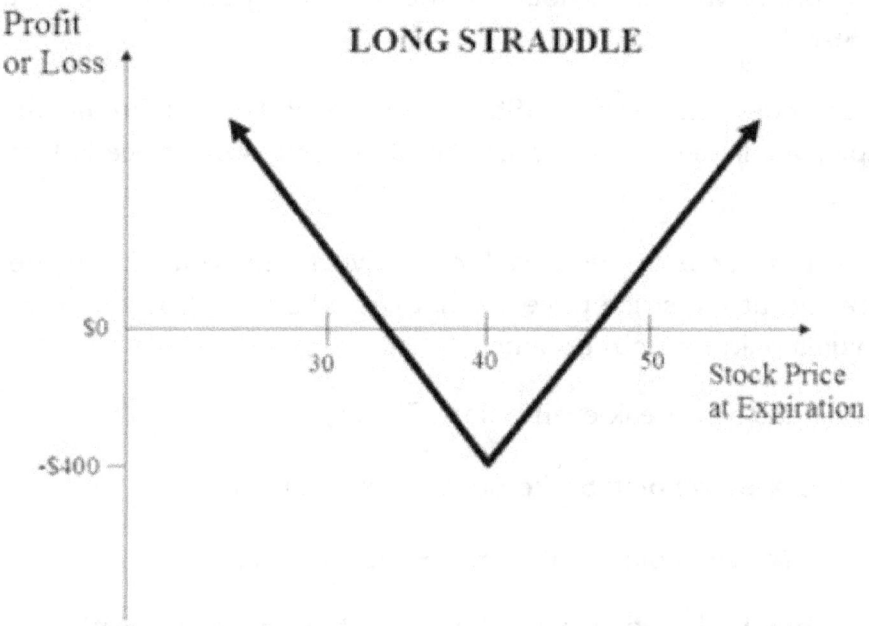

In a Long Straddle, you'll simultaneously buy a Put and Call for the same underlying stock. You're also going to want the same strike price and expiration date. This technique is something that can be utilized with a highly volatile stock. That way, you have the possibility of profiting no matter which way the stock moves. Before we see how this works, let's step back for a second and recall how we determine whether a deal will be profitable. We are looking at this from the buyer's perspective.

In a Call option, you're going to profit when the stock exceeds the strike price. However, you must remember to include the premium in your calculation. If you think a stock will go higher than $54, but you're paying a $1 premium per share, then you will have to invest in a Call option that has a strike price of at least $55.

It's the same game in a Put option, but you're hoping the stock will go below the strike price. So, for our new scenario of buying a Call and a Put at the same strike price and expiration date, we will buy a Put with a strike price of $55. For simplicity, we will stay with a $1 premium.

You need to know the net premium, which will be the sum of the premium from the Call option + the premium from the Put option; in this case, $2.

You can get a profit when one of two conditions are met:

- Price of underlying stock > (Strike price of Call + Net Premium). In our example, you will profit when the amount of the underlying stock is higher than $55 + $2 = $57.

- Price of underlying stock < (Strike price of Put – Net Premium). Using our example, you'll see a profit when the underlying stock price is less than $55- $2 = $53.

The maximum loss for a Straddle will occur when the contract expires with the underlying trading at the strike price. In that case, both contracts expire, and you're out the premiums paid for both options.

A Long Straddle has two break-even points. These are:

- Lower break-even point: Strike price – Net premium

- Upper break-even point: Strike price + Net premium

Remember, you buy both options with the same strike price and expiration date.

Let's look at a simple example. A stock is trading at $100 a share in May. The investor buys a Call with a strike price of $200 that expires on the third Friday in June for $100. The investor also buys a Put with a strike price of $200 that expires on the third Friday of June for $100.

The net premium is $100 + $100 = $200.

Now suppose that on the expiry date, the stock is trading at $300. The Put expires as worthless since the underlying stock price is far above the Put's strike price. However, the investor's Call option expires in-the-money with an intrinsic value of 100 x ($300 - $200) = $10,000. Less the premium, the investor has made $9,800.

On the other hand, suppose that the stock drops in value, and on the expiry, is trading at $50. This time, the Call option expires as worthless. The investor can buy 100 shares for $50 each for a total cost of $5,000. Now he can sell them to exercise the Put option at $200 a share, so he nets $20,000 - $5,000 - $200 = $14,800.

It is a fictitious example, so whether the numbers are realistic or not isn't the point—the point is that the investor will profit no matter what happens to the stock price.

Long Strangle

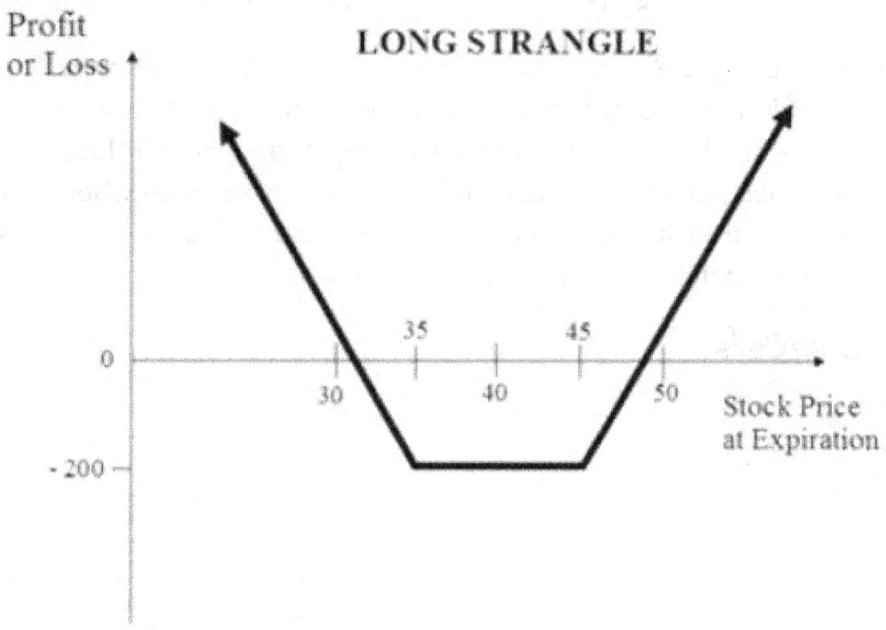

This one will feel like the Long Straddle, but a few differences will help it be own. One of the major differences that you will see is that while the Put and the Call options are still the same and will be on the same asset and expiration date, they will come in with a different strike price for both of these. The price you will use on your Call options will be a bit higher than the price you Put on the Put strike. However, both of these prices are out-of-the-money. This option is less expensive than working with the Long Straddle, but it will be a choice to go with when you think that the asset price will go up or down quite a bit shorter.

In this strategy, you simultaneously purchase a Put and Call option with the expiration date and underlying asset, but at different strike prices. The strike price of the Put option will be lower than the strike price of the Call option. Both options should also be out-of-the-money.

Use this strategy when you believe an underlying asset's price will have a large movement, but you are unsure how direction the move shall be. The losses you incur with this strategy are limited to the cost of the two options. A Long Strangle is typically cheaper than Straddles because the options are purchased out-of-the-money.

The advantage of going with this Long Strangle rather than the Long Straddle is that the amount of premium that you will have to pay for your premiums will be less than what you have to pay with the Long Straddle. However, for the Long Strangle to work, you will need the move in the market to be much bigger to recover your costs.

Traders will profit using the Long Strangle any time they see a sharp move in their stock, similar to using the Long Straddle position, and you still have the potential to make unlimited profits. However, with this strategy, the maximum loss will happen if the stock price settles between the Call and the Put's strike price when you reach the expiry time. In both the Straddle and the Strangle, the maximum loss will be the premiums you paid for the Put and the Call options.

Back Spread w/Calls

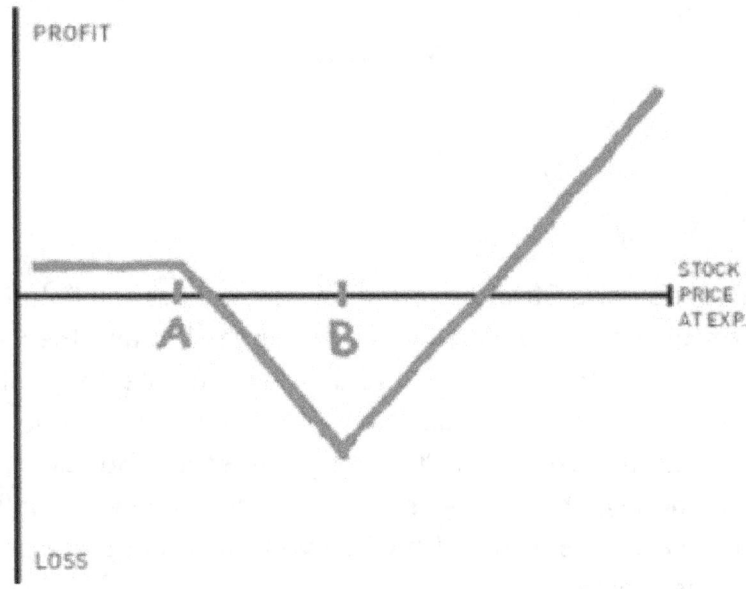

You are required to purchase Calls and the right Calls to create a Call ratio Back Spread. Since it is a ratio Spread, the number of options you execute in each transaction will not be the same. As a rule of thumb, try to purchase two Calls for every Call you write. Always ensure that the total credit for the contracts you've written must be higher than the total debit for the contracts you have acquired.

Back Spread w/Puts

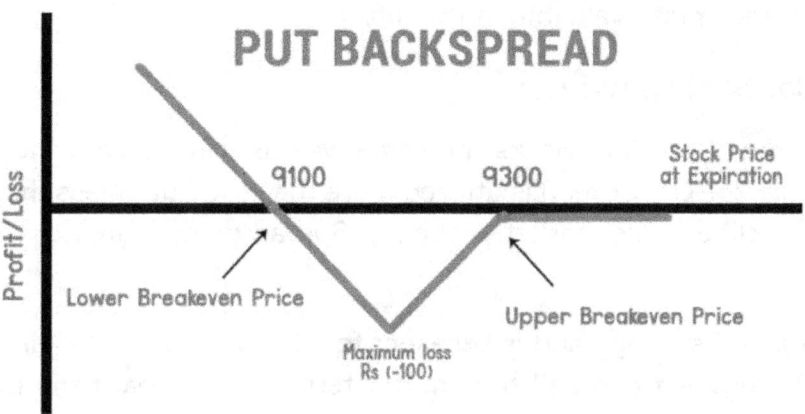

You will earn a profit if the price of the underlying asset moves in either direction; however, your profitability increases if the underlying asset price goes down instead of going up. You are required to purchase Puts and write Puts simultaneously. As is obvious, both of these transactions will be based on the same underlying asset. The only difference is that instead of purchasing an equal number of Puts, you will be purchasing two Puts for every Put you right. The Puts you purchase must be at-the-money while the ones you write must be in-the-money. The expiry date, along with the underlying security, must be the same.

Long Calendar Spread w/Calls

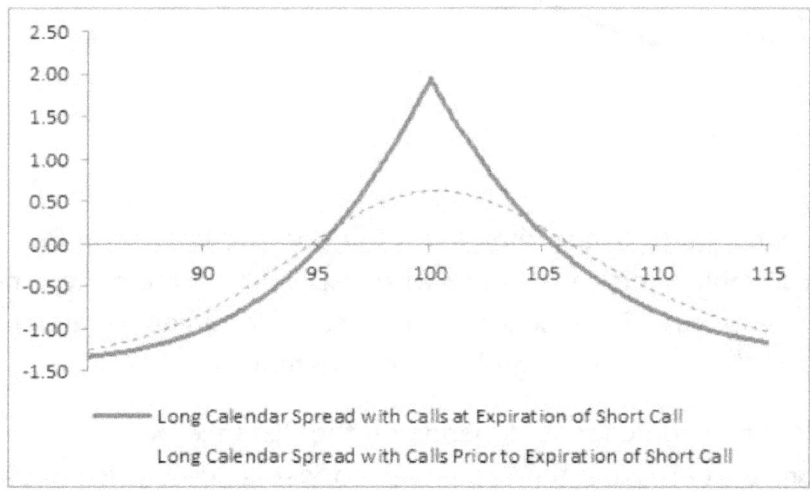

This strategy is meant for a trader who wishes to benefit from the associated assets staying stagnant in the market while also benefiting from the long-term Call position if the stock becomes more valuable in the future.

Long Calendar Spread w/Puts

The Calendar Spread on Puts works the same way as it does with the Call Calendar Spread. Generally, the Call Spread is utilized more than the Put unless there is a greater than expected decline in the market or the Put Spread gives a greater return than the Call Spread.

It is a market-neutral strategy and is excellent for sideways markets. Like with the Call Spread, this strategy aims to sell the shorter-term Put and earn the premium while going long on the longer-term Put.

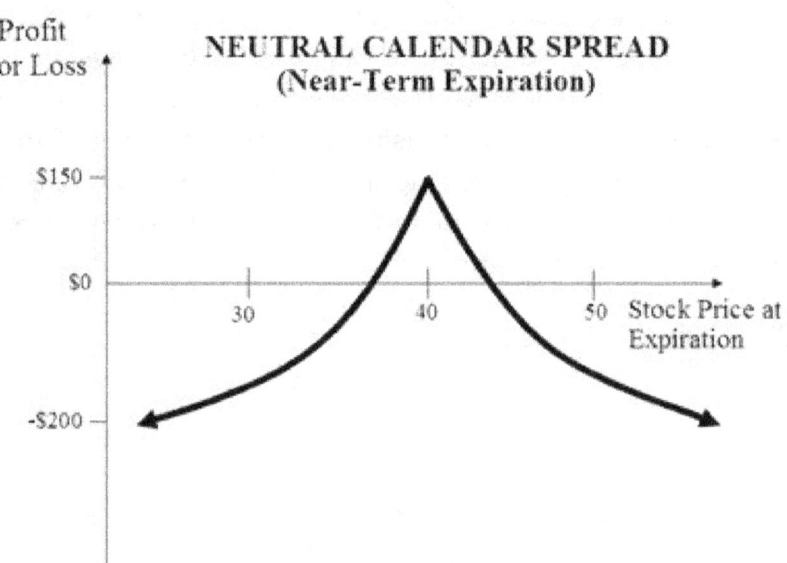

The trade has two legs to it: the short-term Put and the long-term Put. The first step is to identify a suitable short-term Put to write. Generally, if the price is near a support level and you're expecting it to meander a bit before declining in the longer term, you can choose an at-the-money or slightly out-of-the-money option.

The exact strike price you choose depends on the distance between the current price and the support level ahead. If there is a gap, choose a strike price that is beyond the support level. Sticking with our example of AAPL, let's assume it is at a support level that will hold for the short term before folding in the medium term.

Currently, AAPL is trading at $181.30 so let's assume $180 is our support level for the short term. The current month $180 Put is the most suitable to write, and doing this will fetch us a premium of $3.40. The near month $180 Put will cost $5.95 to go long on, and thus, our entry cost of the trade works out to:

Cost of trade entry/Maximum loss per share= Premium paid for near month Put- Premium received for current month meander Put= 5.95-3.4= $2.55 per share.

The maximum reward, just like the Call Calendar Spread, is something that depends on whether or not the stock falls below the support level over the medium term. If it does, you could exercise your near-month option and ride the stock as it declines. Alternatively, you could trade the option itself and save yourself the commissions that arise from exercising it.

The factors to consider for this strategy are the same as the Call Calendar Spread, except this is a bearish version of that strategy. You want to identify a level that the price is likely to remain above for the short-term but will dip below during the medium term.

The reward-risk profile of this trade is excellent, and under the right market conditions, the Calendar Spread is a great strategy to deploy.

It might seem on the surface that a lot of the strategies replicate one another, but their risk profiles are different. So, make sure you work out the numbers before entering them or deciding which one is better. Generally speaking, you can follow the below guidelines to help you decide.

When Calls become expensive, bull Call Spreads work best in the case of a bull market on its last legs. It is to capture whatever moderate level of gains there might be left. Of course, this presumes that you can read the decreasing strength of a trend well enough to deploy it in the first place.

When volatility spikes and there aren't too many downside gains to be acquired in the final stages of a bear market, a Bear Call Spread works the best. Bear markets tend to be shorter than bullish ones since the general public doesn't indulge in the short side. Thus, bear markets don't suffer from the over-enthusiasm that tends to push bull markets longer than expected.

The Bull Put Spread works like a charm in a sideways market when you are certain that the overall trend is still bullish, but currently, the stock is moving sideways or suffering from a bout of counter-trend enthusiasm. It is a good way to earn some income in the meantime and is a far safer option than trying to time a directional entry.

When a bear trend is accelerating to the downside, a Bear Put Spread works the best. You could use this to hedge your positions in a long market, but that's not a trading strategy per se. As it is, using it in the manner described previously is your best bet of making some money off it.

The term comes from how option chains are displayed. The strike prices are listed Vertically, with the Puts and Calls arranged on either side of them. Thus, the lower strike price is above the current price and the higher ones below.

So, by employing two legs on the trade, you're creating a Vertical Spread, as per the option chain table. With a Calendar Spread, you're on the same strike price, but visualizing a calendar, you're moving sideways or Horizontally to the next month. Hence, the term Horizontal Spread.

You also would have noticed how some strategies, upon entry, pay you, and some require an upfront cost. The ones that pay you are Called net credit strategies and the ones that have a cost are Called net debit ones. Net credit strategies pay you your full reward upfront, while net debit ones require you to wait for the maximum reward.

Of course, the flip side is that net debt strategies have you experiencing your full loss upfront instead of net credit ones, where you need to see how it plays out. Take care not to develop a mental bias towards one another. All that matters is the market condition, not which one pays you first or last.

Diagonal Spread w/Calls

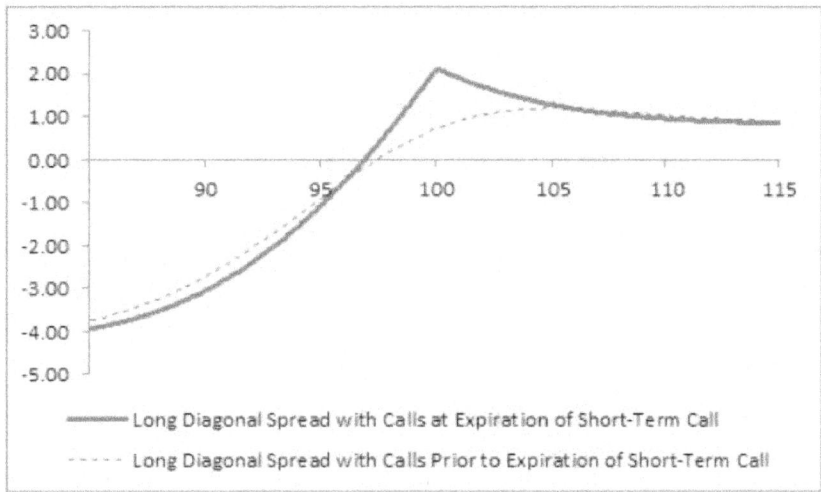

A Diagonal Call is a Spread that allows you to generate monthly income from the stock market and, at the same time, benefit from the strengthening or impairment of stocks. Okay, so how does it work? Just buy a variant that does not expire for many months. You will also sell an option that expires in the previous month.

Let's say you buy a Call option for ten months at $12. Then you sell the Call for the first month with a higher realization price for two months. You can be profitable.

Let's say you sell the first month of ten months each month. You earn $2 each month and sell a total of $20, which is excellent considering you paid $12 for Calls and sold $20. If everything went well, it would be a profit of only 8 or 66% after just ten months.

If stock drops or you receive a Call, you can easily buy the option you sold or sell the purchased option to reduce your losses. The Diagonal Call's beautiful thing is that they allow you to make money when the stock also increases. Let's say the stock gives you a bullish signal for one month, and you think the stock will go up, and you can always decide not to sell the Call this month.

It gives you a standard Calling option that increases with stock prices and is likely to provide you with even more money than if you sold that option in a given month.

Because it's still possible to lose money with a Diagonal Spread, you still need to stop loss and manage risk. Having any strategy will significantly increase your chances. Advisably, only professional traders should consider utilizing Diagonal Call Spread.

Diagonal Spread w/Puts

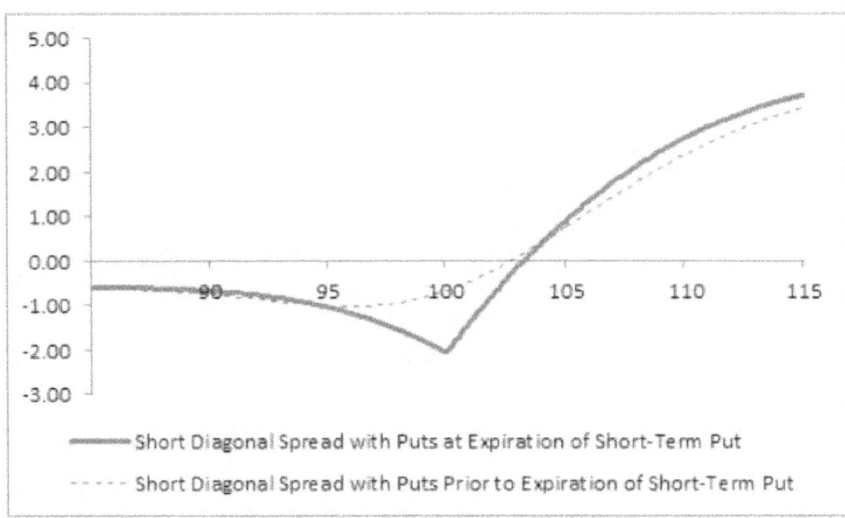

A combination of a Short Calendar, Spread, and Vertical Put Spreads makes up a Diagonal Put Spread. Thus, this strategy often exhibits the attributes of both Spreads. Among such attributes include directionally bearish and short volatility with minimal, zero, or positive time decay. The resultant time decay will depend on the selected expirations and strike price.

To use this strategy, you need to take a bearish position in stock using options. However, it's vital to take an approach with less time decay than a traditional Vertical Put Spread. In comparison to long-dated options, short-dated ones usually decay faster. Consequently, a Diagonal Put Spread possesses less time decay compared to a Vertical Put Spread. However, the similarity between Diagonal Put Spread and Vertical Put Spread is that they utilize various strike prices for directional movement.

When you use a Diagonal Put Spread, the maximum gain will be the difference between the higher strike and lower strike, then subtracted from the premium received. In a situation where the market goes against your strategy, the maximum loss will occur. When the price of the underlying asset reduces significantly, the value of the two options reaches zero. In such a situation, the premium paid upfront will end up as a loss. You can also experience a break-even situation—It is a function of the longer-dated option's price at the due date of the shorter-date option. Here, the break-even usually lies somewhere under the strike of the higher strike option. Finally, considering that the Diagonal Put strategy demands the knowledge of Vertical Put Spread and Calendar Put Spread, it's best recommended for the professional options trader to know both.

Double Diagonal Options Strategy

The Double Diagonal Spread is an options trading strategy that combines a Diagonal Put Spread with a Diagonal Call Spread. The main purpose of constructing this Spread is to benefit from time decay and exploit short positions close to expiration. This way, a trader can generate profits and greatly benefit any long-term positions held in the market. This Spread is also created to profit from the neutral price action of the underlying stock between the two strike prices of the Short Calls. The strategy itself carries limited risk.

Example of Double Diagonal Spread	
Sell 1 28-day XYZ 95 Put at 1.30	1.30
Buy 1 56-day XYZ 100 Put at 3.80	(3.80)
Buy 1 56-day XYZ 100 Call at 4.00	(4.00)
Buy 1 XYZ 110 Call at 1.50	1.50
Net debit =	(5.00)

Strategy Details

The Double Diagonal strategy is constructed by selling a short-term Strangle Spread and a longer-term Straddle purchase. We can take a look at the example provided above to understand this strategy better. In our case, we have a Straddle and Strangle.

There is a 2-month 100 Straddle with 56 days to expiration that is bought, and we also have a Strangle strategy. The 95–110 Strangle is sold and has 28 days or one month to expiration. Risks and profit potentials are limited, and the strategy is set up basically to result in a net debit.

It's an advanced strategy because, in dollar terms, the profit potential is small. Due to the small-dollar amounts for profit potential, you need to ensure that you always get great prices when you open or close positions. You also need to ensure that you engage in large volume trades or a large number of Spreads to keep commissions for the contracts as low as possible.

Maximum Loss and Profit

This option position will see you attain maximum profitability when the underlying stock price equals one of the different strike prices affiliated with the short Strangle. When the price or value of the underlying stock equals that of the Short Call's strike price, then the profit at this point will be exactly equal to the Long Straddle cost minus the cost of commissions charged and the value of the Diagonal Spread.

We consider this point as the apex of maximum profits. The reason is that the Long Call section of the Long Straddle will experience a total price difference with the Short Call that is close to expiration. The stock price at the strike price relates to the Short Put option upon the Strangle option's expiration. It is another point of maximum profit.

It happens because the Long Straddle's Long Put component gains its highest price difference with the Short Put about to expire. Ordinarily, it would be difficult to affirm the maximum profit potential as other factors at play, such as the Long Straddle value, are dependent on volatility levels.

On the other hand, we have the maximum risk possible with this Spread position. The real risk that the position exposes a trader is the same as the Spread's total cost and all commissions due. As a trader, you will lose this entire amount when the Straddle's strike price is equivalent to that of the underlying stock. The Straddle position's price decreases to almost zero so that the entire amount received for the Spread is lost.

Break-even Price at Expiration

This strategy features the main break-even positions. There is one below the Short Put's strike price and another above the Short Call's strike price. As such, the ideal break-even point is equivalent to the price of the underlying stock, where the Long Straddle's value is equivalent to the cost of setting up the Spread minus the Strangles value at expiration.

Generally, it is almost impossible to determine the total loss that will occur or the value at the Strangle's expiration. The reason is that this value relies on the value of the Long Straddle, which in return is a factor of volatility levels.

Loss and profit levels on the Long Straddle position rely largely on the short Strangle expiration dates' estimated value. The estimation is done or computed using the pricing formula Black Scholes Model. It is a pricing formula and makes certain assumptions such as a volatility number of 30%, a total of 28 days or one month to expiration, and zero dividends with an interest rate of 1%.

Proper Market Forecast

As a trader or investor, you need to make the right predictions and forecast the market's behavior. It is crucial for several reasons, mostly because you want to get it right and have profit-making positions. Ideally, the value of the underlying stock should be close to the strike price of the Straddle.

Ordinarily, the price of the underlying security is found near or at the Straddle's strike price. It is the case when you set up the position, so the forecast for this is a neutral price action that occurs in the middle of the two strike prices on the short Strangle.

General Information

The Double Diagonal Spread strategy is the most preferred strategy when the forecast showcases some price activity between the Short Strangle's strike price. In this case, the tradeoff is that we first establish for net debit a Double Diagonal Spread such that it ends with a lower profit opportunity than a Short Strangle.

Remember that you will need to exercise trade discipline and patience to succeed in your trade ventures and maximize profits as a trader. Patience is necessary as the strategy benefits from time decay. At the same time, discipline is essential because the Double Diagonal's profit potential is rather small, so the costs you pay to enter, and exit trades should be minimal. You should also be careful when taking partial profits as these can greatly affect the Spread's performance.

Long Butterfly w/Calls

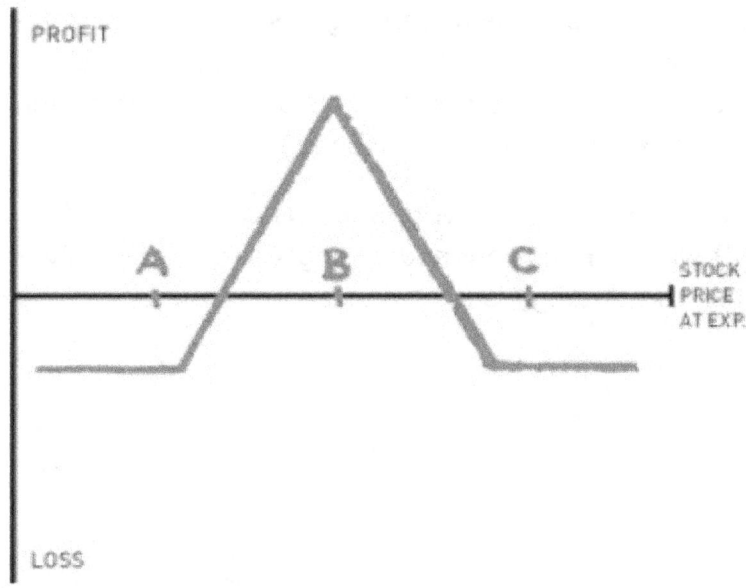

In a Long Butterfly margin using Call options, an investor will combine a bullish margin strategy and a bearish margin strategy that uses three different strike prices for the same underlying asset and the same expiration date.

Long Butterfly w/Puts

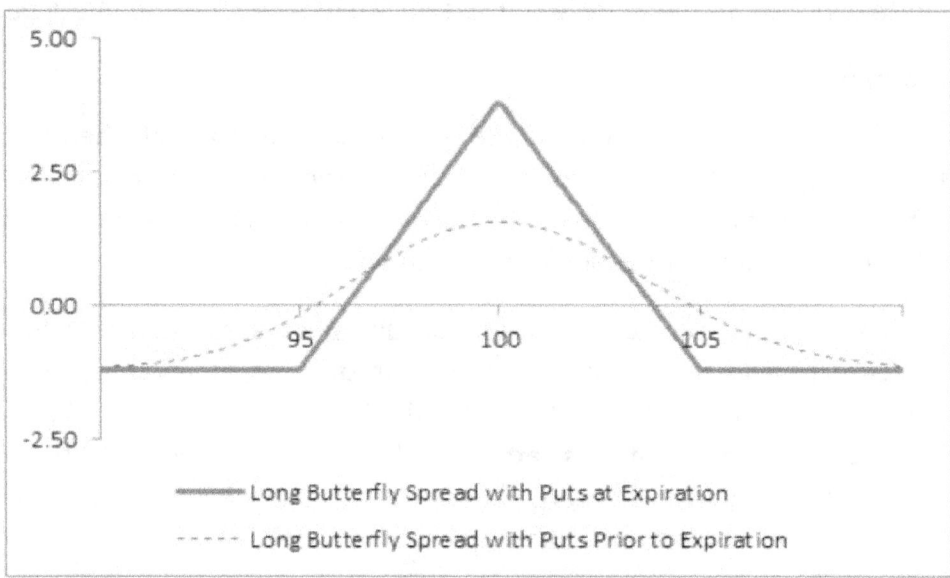

Long Butterfly Spread with Puts at Expiration

Long Butterfly Spread with Puts Prior to Expiration

This strategy consists of buying a Call with a strike price equal to the underlying stock's strike price and selling shares in the underlying stock. Note that one is short an option and long a security. It is not a position that should be undertaken lightly, as it will expose one to credit risk on a payment made on the short options. (this will also expose one to stock risk if it is out-of-the-money.)

The long Butterfly with Puts can be written in one of two ways: (1) writing Calls and selling Puts or (2) writing Puts only and selling Calls. If one only writes Puts while owning stocks, then this strategy is known as an Iron Condor.

Iron Butterfly

An investor would sell an ATM Put in the Iron Butterfly strategy and buy an OTM Put. They would also sell an ATM Call at the very same time and purchase an OTM Call. Both options would be on the same investment product that has the very same expiry date. While this method is identical to a Butterfly Spread, this utilizes both Puts and Calls.

This approach effectively incorporates the sale of an ATM Straddle and the purchase of defensive "wings." The arrangement can also be interpreted as two Spreads. In both Spreads, it is customary to get the same width. The OTM Call covers that long infinite downside. The long OTM Put defends against the negative. Based on the price levels of the options chosen, gain and losses are both restricted to a small range. Investors like this method for the revenue it produces and the greater possibility of a small benefit from a non-volatile stock.

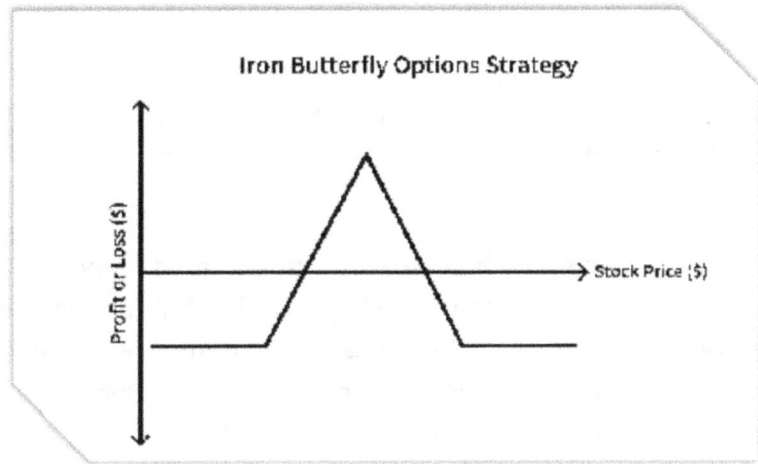

Note in the P&L graph earlier that whenever the stocks stay at the ATM strikes of either the Call and Put, the maximum profit is generated. The cumulative net premium earned is the overall benefit. When the market reaches well above the Long Call strike or under the Long Put strike, excessive loss occurs.

Skip-Strike Butterfly w/Calls

We can describe the Long Skip-Strike Butterfly Spread with Calls as a strategy consisting of four different Call options but three distinct parts. When it comes to advanced Call options, we like to consider four different strike prices. These prices are A, B, C, and D, where D is the largest price, and A is the lowest.

A trader creates a Long Skip-Strike Butterfly Spread with a Call options strategy by:

- purchasing at the strike price A a Call option

- avoiding strike price C and selling two Call options at strike price B

- buying two Call options at strike price B,

- buying at the strike price D an additional Call option.

All the different strike prices are equidistant, and the Call options have similar expiration dates.

Example of Long Skip-Strike Butterfly Spread with Calls	
Buy 1 XYZ 90 Calls at 8.00	(8.00)
Sell 2 XYZ 100 Calls at 4.90	9.80
Buy 1 XYZ 110 Calls at 0.90	(0.90)
Net credit =	0.90

Example

From the example of the long Skip-Strike Butterfly Spread with Call options, the trader buys a 90-Call option and then sells two Calls at 100 before purchasing another Call option at 110.

The example shown above clearly indicates that this is an advanced strategy because its costs are quite high. The maximum risk possible is relatively high in terms of percentage. The costs incurred include numerous commissions that have to be paid based on the three distinct strike prices. Also, part of the costs is the three bid-ask Spreads incurred when opening and closing positions. That's why traders need to ensure that all positions opened or closed are considered a good price. Commissions should also be carefully considered because they are likely to impact profits.

Maximum Profit

You will experience a maximum profit with this strategy when profit equates to the difference in price between the initial net credits plus the strike price associated with the two Short Calls, then subtracted from the lowest strike price or the Long Call option. It can also be equivalent to the strategy's lowest strike price minus strike price associated with two Short Calls minus the commissions and the initial net debt.

You will receive the maximum profit when the underlying stock's price at expiration is equivalent to a strike price associated with Short Calls. For instance, in our example above, the difference between Short Calls' strike price & the lowest strike price is $5.00, while the net credit at the onset is $0.25 but without any commissions. In our case, therefore, the amount is $5.25 inclusive of commissions.

Maximum Risk with this Strategy

When trading options using this strategy, you can expect the maximum risk equivalent to the difference in price between the Long Call or the highest strike price & strike price associated with two Short Calls minus the highest possible profit.

Sometimes, positions are held for either net debit/net credit. In the above example, the situation is a net credit. As a result, we can expect the maximum possible loss to occur when the underlying stock's value, at expiration, is equivalent to or greater than the largest strike price.

In the situation above, we note that the difference between the largest strike price & Short Calls is $10.00, while the maximum profit as noted above is $5.25 without commissions. As such, the maximum possible loss in our situation is $10.00 - $5.25 = $4.75.

Skip Strike Butterfly w/Puts

The Skip Strike Butterfly with Puts is an advanced options trading strategy with four distinct Put options and is a three-part strategy. This specific Skip Butterfly Spread with a Put option is created by purchasing a Put option at strike price A, leaving out strike price B, disposal of two Put options at the strike price C, and finally purchasing another Put option at strike price D. This strategy approach considers four different strike prices: A, B, C, and D, where A is the lowest price, while D happens to be the highest. In this instance, the strike prices are equally spaced from each other, while all the Put options have similar expiration dates.

Example of Long Skip-Strike Butterfly Spread with Puts	
Buy 1 XYZ 110 Calls at 8.20	(8.20)
Sell 2 XYZ 100 Calls at 4.70	9.40
Buy 1 XYZ 90 Calls at 0.90	(0.90)
Net credit =	0.30

In the example above, we observe that a single Put option at a strike price of $90 is purchased, two Put options at the strike price of $100 sold, and a Put option at the strike price of $110 bought. The $105 strike price sees no activity and is skipped. The layout in the position above is set out for a net credit, which means maximum risk and maximum possible profits are both limited.

We consider this strategy to be an advanced one as the highest possible risk is large percentage-wise, and the expenses of setting up the Spread are also high. The strategy has numerous commissions that have to be paid, three strike prices, and three bid-ask Spreads. It is crucial to ensure that positions are opened at what are considered good prices and ensure commissions' cost as these can be rather costly.

Maximum Profits and Loss

When you implement this strategy, the maximum benefit you can earn is equivalent to the difference in price between the initial net credit added to the two Short Puts and the highest strike price, or less than the initial net debit and all commissions due. When the stock price is equivalent to the actual Short Puts' strike price upon expiration, you will get this benefit. The biggest loss you can incur is equivalent to the price difference between the lowest strike price and the two Short Puts minus the total benefit possible.

Inverse Skip Strike Butterfly w/Calls

The purpose of this specific options strategy is to benefit when the underlying stock's price rises higher than that of the largest strike price with almost no risks should the underlying stocks' price drop below the smallest strike price. Profit-taking is subject to taking the measured risk of a large percentage loss should the underlying stock's price trade close to Long Calls' strike price.

Definition

Inverse Skip Strike Butterfly with Calls is also Called the Short Skip Strike Butterfly Spread. It is an options trading strategy with three distinct parts and with four Call options. As with other advanced options strategies, we assume a situation with four strike prices: A, B, C, and D. We create the inverse Skip Strike Butterfly strategy with Call options by selling a Call at the strike price D, doing away with strike price C, purchasing two Call options at strike price B, and selling a single Call at strike price A. In this instance, all the strike prices are equally spaced out while the Call options have similar expiration dates. It is an advanced options trading strategy as the highest risk possible percentage-wise is high, and the associated costs of setting up the strategy are significant. There are plenty of commissions that have to be paid based on the three strike prices. In addition to this, three bid-ask Spreads are incurred during the opening and closing of positions. That's why it is advisable to ensure that positions are opened and closed at prices considered good.

Maximum Profits and Maximum Loss

As an options trader implementing this specific strategy, your maximum possible benefit is generally equivalent to the largest strike price minus total possible risk less the two Long Calls' strike price.

There are two possible outcomes when a position is being established on the market for a net debit. One situation occurs when the underlying stock's price is equivalent to or above the largest strike price, the total profit or benefit obtainable will be obtained. However, when the stock's price is the same at the expiration as the lowest strike price, all the Calls will worthlessly expire, and in this instance, the original net debit used to set up the positions will be lost.

When you establish this position in the market for a net credit, you will realize maximum profitability when the underlying stock's price, at expiration, is higher than or equivalent to the highest strike price.

A maximum possible loss that you can incur on this trade is the same as the difference between two Long Calls' strike price & the smallest strike price added to an original debt incurred when setting up the position, or less the initial credit incurred as the commissions paid.

Inverse Skip Strike Butterfly w/Puts

The inverse Skip Strike Butterfly Spread strategy with Put options contains four Put options and is essentially a three-component strategy. As with other complex options strategies, we consider a situation with four distinct strike prices. These are strike prices A, B, C, and D, where A is the largest strike price and D the smallest.

We create an inverse Skip Strike Butterfly with Puts by selling a single strike Put option at strike price A, leaving out strike price B altogether, purchasing dual Puts at price strike C, and eventually selling a single Put option at strike price D. In this instance, the four strike prices - A, B, C, and D - are equally spaced while all the Puts share a similar expiration date.

Purpose

This specific advanced options trading strategy aims to benefit from the decline of a stock price to levels below the lowest strike price, and with almost no risk should the stock price increase to levels way above the highest strike price. Simultaneously, taking on the risk of bigger losses should the underlying stock's price traded at levels close to the Long Puts' strike prices.

Example of Inverse Skip-Strike Butterfly Spread with Puts	
Sell 1 XYZ 110 Put at 8.20	8.20
Buy 2 XYZ 105 Puts at 4.50	(9.00)
Sell 1 XYZ 95 Put at 0.90	0.70
Net debit =	(0.10)

In the example indicated above, we sell on 95 Put, avoid the 100 strike price, purchase two 105 Puts, and sell a 110 Put. As such, we establish a position for a net debit. In this instance, there is a limitation on both profitability and losses, and the setup results in a net debit.

We can observe that this is an advanced strategy as the costs incurred to set up the position are relatively high, and also, the total risk the trader is exposed to is also high. Please note that multiple commissions have to be paid out. Three strike prices also require funds and bids and ask Spreads to be funded when closing and opening. You should consider all the commissions per contract because these can have a huge impact on profitability.

Maximum Profits and Maximum Loss

In this instance, you will enjoy maximum profits with the difference between the dual Long Puts' strike price & the lowest strike price minus the maximum risk.

Now, the established position in our example above is for a net debit. In our case, we realize a maximum profit when, at expiration, the "stock's price" is lower than or equivalent to the smallest strike price. When we look at the situation above, we can work out the profit as the strike price of Long Puts minus total possible risk fewer commissions. In our case, the total profit possible is 10.00 − 5.35 = 4.65.

Christmas Tree Butterfly w/Calls

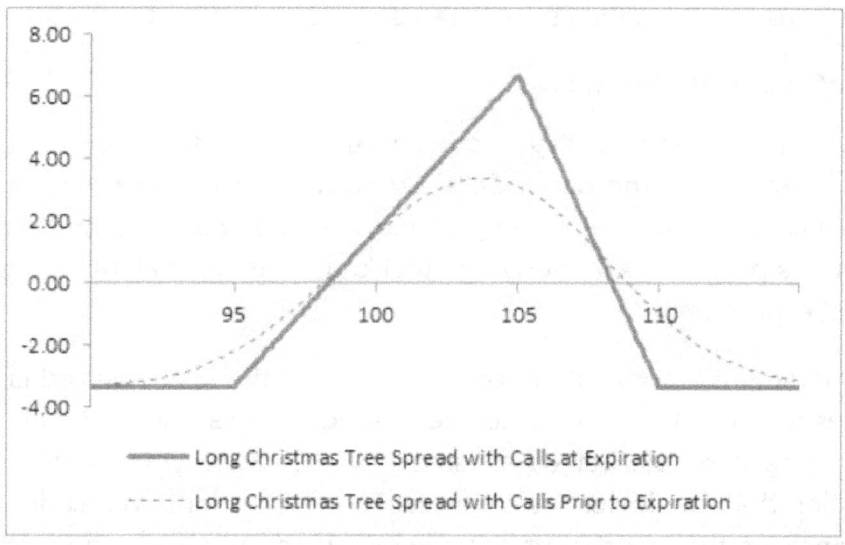

The long Christmas tree Spread Butterfly with Call options is ideally a strategy made up of three distinct components with six different Calls. In the instance of four distinct strike prices, A, B, C, and D, where D is the largest strike price and A is the smallest, we can use these to help set up our strategy. We also work with the situation where all the strike prices are spaced out equally and where the Call options share similar expiration dates.

Although it's very much similar to the traditional Butterfly strategy, the difference is that you will implement this strategy together with an underlying stock that's trading at the strike price A. As a trader, you need to be on the lookout for small upward movements.

To create this position, we will purchase dual Calls at strike price D, sell three options Calls at strike price C, not use strike price B, and then purchase a single Call option at strike price A. Remember that all the Calls in this strategy feature similar expiration dates and the strike prices are all equidistant.

The position could be established for a net debit. Also, one needs to consider this strategy to be an advanced one because costs are rather high. The strategy consists of multiple bid and ask Spreads and numerous commissions that have to be paid when opening and closing positions.

Due to the high costs, it is advisable to ensure that all positions are entered at good prices because the commissions and costs will affect profitability. It is also why it is a good idea to consider the commission's rates charged per contract.

Maximum Profits and Maximum Loss

When you apply this trading strategy, you can expect to receive maximum profitability, which is equivalent to all the Short Calls' strike price minus the lowest strike price, subtracting all costs incurred in setting up the strategy and all commissions charged. You will earn this profit if the underlying stock's price is equivalent to the strike price at Short Calls' expiration.

On the other hand, maximum risk or loss will be when the loss incurred is equal to the total expenses sustained in setting up the strategy. There are generally pathways to the maximum possible risk. Let us assume that the underlying stock's price is way under expiration than the lowest strike price. The Call options will expire worthless in such an instance, so the investment or payments made to set up the positions will all be lost.

On the other hand, we can suffer a maximum loss when, at expiration, the underlying stock's value is higher than the largest strike price; the Call options will be in-the-money so that the position will expire with a value of zero. In this case, all the costs incurred, including commissions paid, will disappear.

Christmas Tree Butterfly w/Puts

The long Christmas tree options Spread with Put options can be defined as an options trading strategy consisting of three components and six individual components. Let us assume a situation where we have four different strike prices named strike price A, B, C, and D, with A being the lowest and D the largest. We can create the Long Christmas Tree Spread option by:

- purchasing two Put options at strike price A

- selling triple Puts at strike price B

- skip strike price C for now, and

- buying a single Put option at price strike D.

In our case, the strike prices are all equally spaced from each other, and the options all have the same expiration date. Traders create and use this strategy to benefit from stocks' neutral price action with minimal risk when being very close to Short Put options' strike price. We can view this strategy as an advanced one generally because the stocks are priced highly.

Close observation reveals that multiple bid-ask Spreads and commissions are paid for the six options and three strike prices.

Example of Long Christmas Tree Spread with Puts	
Buy 1 XYZ 110 Put at 8.20	(8.20)
Sell 3 XYZ 100 Puts at 2.00 each	6.00
Buy 2 XYZ 90 Puts at 0.75 each	(1.50)
Net debit =	(3.70)

In our example above, we note that our position is established for a net debit. We also note that both the maximum risk and potential for profit are limited. Also, the position requires one 110 Put option is purchased, three 100 Put options are sold, the 105 strike price is skipped, and a pair of 90 Puts are purchased.

Maximum Profits and Maximum Losses

When you apply this strategy, your best profit outlook is similar to the difference in price between the three Short Put's strike prices and the Long Put strike price minus the cost of setting up the strategy, including commissions. You will make this profit when at expiration, the underlying stock's value is equivalent to the Short Put's strike price.

A maximum risk or largest loss only includes the total cost of setting up the entire strategy, which includes purchasing the options and the commissions due. There are generally two possible outcomes for a maximum loss. The first instance when the "underlying stock value's price" at expiration falls below that of the lowest or smallest strike price. In this case, all the Puts will be in-the-money, and at expiration, the Spread position will be worth nothing.

On the other hand, when the underlying stock's value is higher than the largest strike price at expiration, then the Put options will worthlessly expire, the cost of setting up the position, and the commissions due will all be expenses incurred for no reason.

Long Condor Spread w/Calls

We can define the Long Condor Spread with Call options as an options strategy with four distinct components. This strategy is created by selling a Call option with a higher strike price, purchasing a Call option at a lower strike price, purchasing another Call option with a much higher strike price, and selling another Call option at an even higher strike price. All the Calls applicable in this strategy share similar expiration dates, while the strike prices are all equally spaced out. The strategy's main purpose is to profit the trader from the neutral stocks' price action between the dual strike prices in the middle of the position. This position has limited risks. Therefore, you will need to ensure that the underlying security's value at expiration is somewhere in the middle of the two Short Call strikes. There is another way of viewing this strategy. You can think of this strategy as a Debit Spread or a Bull Call Option Spread in-the-money. It is coupled with a Credit Spread or a Bear Call Spread that is out-of-the-money. The Bull Call Spread is at a lower strike price compared to the Bear Call Spread. You invest in this type of option when you hope for very little or no movement in the underlying stock. As such, you can expect to profit and benefit when the stock price lies between the dual Short Call strikes upon expiration.

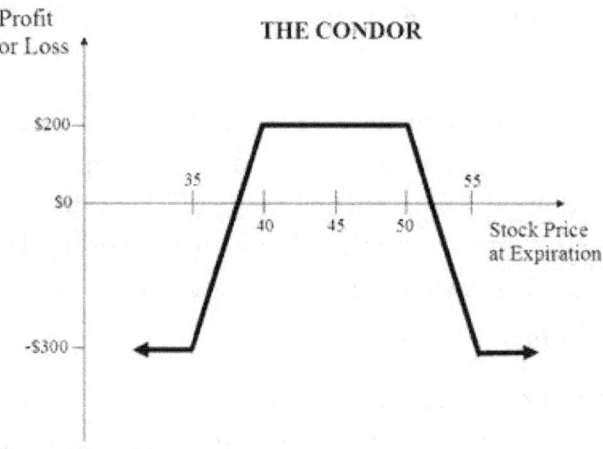

Profit and Losses Outlook

The Long Condor Spread with Call options strategy is generally set up for a net debit with both losses and benefits limited. You can expect maximum profits when the lower strike Long Call has an equivalent value to its highest possible value.

The profit is calculated as the difference between the two strike prices minus the cost of setting up the position, including commissions. The risk of maximum loss occurs when you suffer a loss of all the costs incurred in setting up the position, including all the commissions that need to be paid.

You will incur this total loss when the underlying stock's value is higher than the expiration's largest strike price. Upon expiration of the Spread position, the strategy will expire worthlessly, and all the money put into acquiring positions and all commissions paid will all be lost.

Break-even Price Upon Expiration

You have two break-even points with this position. There is the upper break-even position, and then there is the lower break-even position. The point wherein the underlying stock's value is equivalent to the largest strike price minus the costs incurred in setting up the position is the upper break-even point. We also have the lower break-even point, which occurs when the underlying stock's price is similar to the smallest strike price and all commissions.

Best Market Forecast

Traders often want to capitalize on positions they take in the market. If you implement this strategy, you can expect to enjoy the best returns when the stock price at expiration is between the center strike prices. You should be able to forecast a neutral movement of the stock price within the highest profit levels.

When the underlying stock's value lies below or above the accepted range for the highest profit at establishing the position, traders should predict the direction in which the underlying stock will move to enter the determined range for maximum benefit.

Strategy

If a trader forecasts a stock's movement in the region of maximum possible benefit, then Calls's Long Condor Spread option is the best strategy to apply. Generally, the Long Condor Spread strategy benefits from time decay. Therefore, with little market movement, this kind of setup can be quite profitable.

However, the chances or risks of losing out on this strategy are limited. As a trader, you are only going to lose the money invested. It is unlike other strategies such as the short Strangle and the Short Straddle. Compared to the short Straddle strategy and the short Strangle, the Long Condor Spread tends to have very limited profit potential. Another aspect of this position is that Condor Spread commissions are significantly higher than those of other strategies such as the Strangle and Straddle.

This Long Condor Call option strategy and Long Condors, in general, are rather sensitive to volatility. When volatility increases, then the value of Condor Call options tends to fall, while it increases when there is little volatility. Many traders prefer placing such positions just before earnings reports because options volatility tends to drop significantly after such reports.

In instances where traders time their positions accurately, the potential profits are significantly high. Simultaneously, the risks involved are very limited and only affect the funds invested in setting up the position and commissions paid. The stock's value must stay in the middle of the upper strike price & the lower strike price to successfully implement this strategy. Losses will be suffered when the stock value exceeds either of these strike prices.

Sometimes, volatility tends to be constant with little or no movement. In such cases, the Long Condor Spread with Call options will generally not experience a price increase. As such, profits will not be visible until the position is just about to expire and the stock value is somewhere between the two strike prices. It sharply contrasts the short Strangle and the Short Straddle.

When there is little or no volatility in the underlying stock, some profit will be visible even as expiration dates draw nigh. This, however, depends mostly on the price being in between the two strike prices.

Trading Discipline and Patience Are Essential

When you place such advanced trade strategies, you need to remember trading discipline, be patient, and let the strategy play out. Patience is a virtue that is necessary when executing this trade as it involves a strategy whose success is dependent on time decay. On the other hand, Trading discipline is crucial as small alterations in the underlying value price are likely to occur. These can greatly impact the overall price of the Condor position.

Long Condor Spread w/Puts

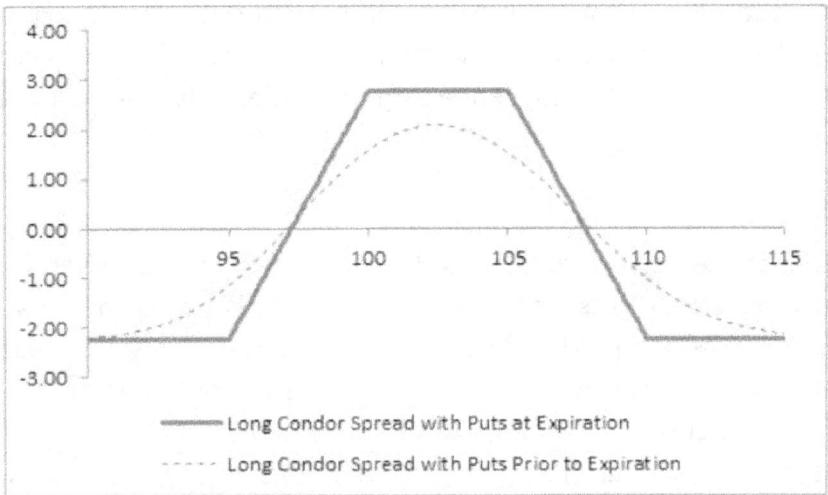

Yet another Condor Spread strategy is this Long Condor Spread with Put options. It is an options trading strategy that consists of four distinct parts. As a trader, you will come up with this Spread strategy by:

- selling a Put option that has a lower strike price than purchasing a single Put option at high strike prices

- selling yet another Put option at an even lower strike price, and then

- purchasing another Put option at a lower strike price.

As in all cases, all the Puts in this strategy share the same expiration date, while all the strike prices are spaced out at equal distances. We establish this strategy for a net debit and note that the profitability and loss risks are both limited. It means you can only earn so much through this strategy but only losing the money you put in should the strategy flop.

Maximum Profits and Maximum Loss

If you implement this strategy, you will reap maximum benefit should the underlying stock's price lie in the middle of two middle strike prices upon expiring the strategy. You will suffer the maximum loss in the same breath when the underlying stock's value is below the smallest strike price figure or above the largest strike price as soon as the expiration date is attained. We consider this to be an advanced strategy as the costs of setting up positions are high and because the possible profits are pretty low.

Setting up costs are high basically because there are four different options as well as four strike prices. You will also be required to pay multiple commissions, as well as bid-ask Spreads during closing and opening positions. That's why it is highly recommended that positions close and open at prices are deemed acceptable. As a trader, you need to consider only engaging in trades with reasonable risk versus rewards ratios.

Total Possible Risk

As with all other strategies, there is some level of risk involved. When it comes to the Long Condor Spread with Puts, the total risk possible is equal to the strategy's total cost plus any commissions paid. In essence, it is equal to only the costs incurred in setting up the position. However, there are two possible outcomes in this strategy for the total loss to be incurred. The first situation is when the underlying stock's price is much higher than the value at the highest strike price's expiration. In this instance, the Put options are going to expire worthlessly. The other situation is where the underlying security's price is much lower than the strike price with the lowest expiration value. When this situation occurs, all the options will be in-the-money, and as such, this Spread will, at expiration, have a net value of zero. In this case, you will suffer a maximum loss equivalent to the full cost of setting up the position and all the commissions paid.

The Break-even Price at Expiration

Our situation also has what is known as the break-even price upon expiration. This strategy includes dual break-even. These break-even points include the lower break-even point & the upper break-even point. When the cost of setting up the position, including all commissions added to the lowest strike price, equals the price of the underlying stock, the lower break-even point occurs. You also have the upper break-even point where the difference between the cost of setting up the position and the highest strike price is equivalent to the underlying stock's value at expiration.

Market Forecast

For this Long Condor Spread strategy to earn you maximum profit, the stock price at expiration will have to be between the center strike prices. For the accurate forecast that ensures you achieve this, you will need to have a neutral price action for the underlying stock and the highest profitability range. In case the price of the underlying stock is below or above the highest possible profitability range when setting up the position, you will require the forecast to point towards a direction stock price movement with the direction headed in the range of maximum profitability. Long

Condor Spreads generally react to volatility: they are extremely sensitive to dynamic volatility. When volatility of the underlying stock rises, then Condor Spread's net value will drop, while Spread's net value will rise should the volatility of the underlying stock fall.

Some traders set up Long Condor positions after predictions and forecasts of falling volatility. Now, options are sensitive to volatility.

CHAPTER 3:

Vertical Spread

When it comes to Spread trading, there are two categories all types of trades fit into. These are Vertical Spreads and Horizontal Spreads. The names sound fancy but understanding how they work isn't anywhere near as complicated.

These types of trades do crank the complexity level up a bit. If the Collar took things up a notch from Covered Calls, Spread trades do the same with the Collar. As beneficial as Collars and Covered Calls are, one major disadvantage is that those strategies pose a danger to the trader.

They require a long stock purchase. For a Covered Call, this is an investment, while for a Collar, it can be speculative or an investment. Whatever the designation, there's no escaping the fact that long stock investment requires a lot of money. What if you wish to emulate Thales' example and get in on low capital values?

It is what the Spread strategies address. Options give us the flexibility to play around with the way price moves, and as you'll see, Spread trades encompass taking advantage of a wide variety of market behavior.

Bull Call Spreads

The first type of Vertical Spread we'll be looking at is the Bull Call Spread. It is a bullish trading strategy and works best in the middle portions of trending markets. I'll address why this is so. For now, keep in mind that while this is a bullish strategy, it works best when bullishness is beginning to slow down and you observe the ranges getting larger.

You can use this in the earlier, more forceful, part of trends, but this isn't the most efficient use of it. In those portions, you're better off simply buying a Call and letting its premium rise. The Covered Call works well in those envlronments too.

Either way, the Bull Call Spread has two legs to it. You will be buying one Call and selling another. Thus, the Long Call leg of the trade covers the Short Call. Let's take a look at the legs in more details.

Trade Legs

The first leg you should establish is the Long Call leg. It needs to be an at-the-money or slightly out-of-the-money Call that you're sure will move into the money soon. The objective is to use this leg to make the majority of the profit in this trade. In essence, you're substituting the long stock position from the previous two strategies with a Long Call position.

Establishing a long stock position meant that you needed to protect it somehow, which is why we had to incorporate the third leg in the Collar case. With the Covered Call, given the investment nature of the trade, downside protection is moot since you'll be holding onto it for the long term anyway, and the objective is to hold onto your investment no matter how much it dips (assuming the dip isn't catastrophic.)

The second leg of the Bull Call Spread is the Short Call. It is written out-of-the-money at a point where you think the price will advance to, even if it does so sluggishly. Much like with every other strategy we've looked at, you want both of these options to expire at least 30 days or more from the trade date. It helps you capture and avoid the risk of time decay.

Like the Collar, the Bull Call Spread can be adjusted, and its greatest power lies in a good adjustment. It allows you to remain in the market at a low cost. Adjustments depend on what the market scenario looks like. You should deploy this when bullishness is starting to be challenged by bearishness, and thus, you will enter with the knowledge that the trend is still strong, but there are some headwinds ahead.

You should place your Short Call at a level beyond the most relevant resistance ahead. Once price breaches this level, you should move it a few points higher to where the next resistance level could potentially be, and so on. Alternatively, if you feel that the counter-trend presence is becoming far too much, you could let the market take you out of the position, close your long, and cover your short position.

Bull Put Spread

The Bull Put Spread strategy seeks to take advantage of the same set of market conditions that the Bull Call Spread seeks. So, what is the difference between the two? Aside from the obvious fact that one strategy uses Calls and the other uses Puts, there are many subtleties that you ought to be aware of.

The strategies do not contradict one another, in case you're wondering. Think of it as having two choices to pursue depending on what market conditions look like. If you're wondering how to determine the ideal conditions for each strategy, then the first step is to take a look at the Bull Put Spread and understand how it works.

Trade Legs

Like the Bull Call, the Bull Put is a two-legged trade. The first leg involves establishing a Long Put position out-of-the-money and is below a strong support level. This Long Put is what caps your downside risk in case things go wrong. In addition to this, the Long Put also covers the next leg.

It is a Short Put that is written near or at-the-money. This leg is the primary profit-driving instrument for the trade. I want to point out that the Puts' structure and positioning are very different from the Calls. With the Bull Call Spread, you were capping your maximum gain on the trade by writing an OTM Call.

Here you're not capping any gains and are capping your loss via a trade leg. In the Bull Call Spread, your maximum loss was automatically capped as a part of the trade structure. You could argue that this is happening here, but it's pretty clear how the strategies that do this are very different.

The next major point of difference is in the results trade entry gives you. The Bull Call is net debt trade, but the Bull Put is a net credit trade. Net debt trades have you realize your maximum loss upon trade entry. With net credit trades, you realize your maximum gain upon entry. It means you earn your maximum profit on entry, and if all goes well, your options will maintain themselves.

Like the Bull Call Spread, you can adjust the trade depending on market conditions. Given that your upside is not capped, adjustments will need to be made primarily if the market turns downwards and if you see your Puts move into the money. In this case, you will need to readjust the Spread lower and exit your primary position. Thus, the Bull Put strategy's adjustment scenarios aren't as varied as they are in the others we've seen so far.

If the trade works in your favor, you can establish a higher Spread using the same principles you used to establish the initial one.

Bear Call Spread

If you can use Call Spreads to take advantage of bullish conditions, you can use them to take advantage of bearish ones as well. In case you're wondering, it is possible to do this with Puts too, and much like what we saw with the Bullish Spreads, you have a choice of using either Call or Put Spreads to do this. For now, let's take a look at Bear Call Spreads.

The Bear Call Spread has two legs to it, much like the Bull Spreads do. As the name suggests, you'll be setting up Calls as part of this strategy. Let's take a deeper look at the two legs now.

Trade Legs

The first leg you want to establish is a Long Call position. The Long Call is placed at a level above a resistance zone and is the leg that limits your risk. The Call itself is placed out-of-the-money. The further away the Call is, the greater your risk in the trade is.

The second leg to establish is the primary profit-driving leg of this trade. It is a Short Call you will write as close to the money as possible. This level's exact placement is tricky since you don't want it to move into the money. If it does, you'll have to wind up both the trade legs and take your maximum loss amount.

Bear Call Spreads are net credit trades, which means you'll capture your entire gain upon trade entry. As such, like other options trading strategies we've seen thus far, you don't need to do anything special to maintain the trade. You can adjust it as well, but given that this is a net credit trade, there isn't much you can do to adjust beyond working out another Spread level if the original trade doesn't work out.

Bear Put Spread

The Bear Put Spread is the bearish cousin of the Bull Call Spread in that it is a net debit trade that seeks to capture more of the upside in a bearish movement. By now, hopefully, you've got the hang of how Vertical Spread trades are set up, so let's quickly run through how this trade works.

Like the other three, it has two legs: A Long Put and a Short Put. The Long Put is established at-the-money or as near to the money as possible and is the primary profit driver in this trade. The Short Put is written out-of-the-money, a few levels below, and functions as a profit target of sorts.

Like with the Bull Call Spread, this trade aims to capture as much of the market movement as possible. Hence, adjustments play an important role here. Once the market moves close to your Short Call, you can adjust your target downwards and move your Long Call leg up.

The timeline for this trade is the same as that of the others. You're looking at establishing options at least 30 days or so away from the trade entry date to avoid or capture as much of the time decay as possible. Using our TSLA example with a market price of $478.15, let's assume that we write the TSLA 450 option expiring a month from now.

It will net us $23.90 in premiums. We can go long on the 475 Put, which will cost us $36.05. Thus, the net debit on the trade and our maximum loss is $12.15. Our maximum gain is limited to the OTM Put's strike price, and this is $25.

CHAPTER 4:

Horizontal Spread

Here are some Horizontal Spreads that traders should know about.

Calendar Call Spread Strategy

The Spreads we've seen thus far have been what are Called Vertical Spreads. It implies how they show up on the option chain, where strike prices are listed on top of one another. By shorting one and buying another, you're earning the difference in the two's prices and hence the term 'Spread.'

Vertical Spreads require you to trade options within the same expiration month. The Calendar Spreads involve buying and selling options from different expiration months. The Call Calendar Spread is a bullish strategy that can be used to great effect, as we'll see.

Execution

The calendar Call Spread consists of two legs:

A current month or short-term Short Call

A near month or longer-term Long Call

The idea is that while the stock takes its time to make it to the longer (time frame) Call's strike price, you might as well collect the premium on the Short Call in the meantime. The instrument for profit is the Long Call, which captures the upward movement in the stock.

The longer-term Call can be from the near month or something from the longer cycle. The choice is yours. The only consideration here is the liquidity since you don't want to be trading in an instrument with a huge Spread thanks to low demand or trading volume. As long as the liquidity is fine and Spreads are low or manageable, you should be fine.

As your first step to implementing the trade, you will purchase an at or in-the-money Call in anticipation of the move upwards. The Short Call is at a level you think the price will not reach within that time frame. The idea is to earn the premium from the Short Call and the Long Call's capital gain. If this trade works out, it is as close to a win-win as you can get in the markets. Let's see how the math works with AMZN.

Let's say our Long Call is from the near month. The price we'll pay for the 1830 Call, which is nearest to the market price and in-the-money, is $63.65. For our Short Call, let's say there is a medium-level resistance at 1840, which AMZN will have to work to get past and is unlikely to do this by the end of the month.

The premium we earn on this Call is $36.30.

The cost of entry = Cost of Long Call - premium earned from Short Call = 63.65-36.3 = $27.35 per share.

Maximum loss = cost of entry

There are many scenarios for calculating the maximum gain, as you can imagine, since this depends on whether the short-term Call ever moves into the money. Whatever the scenario, you will have to subtract your cost of entry from the final gain.

Horizontal Spreads are thus different from Vertical Spreads, thanks to their open-ended nature. It will take some getting used to, but with time, you'll find that they tend to be far more rewarding if you can get your analysis correct.

Put Calendar Spread

The Horizontal Put Spread is similar in premise to the Call Calendar Spread, except it seeks to take advantage of a bearish market. The structure of the trade is also similar to the Call. It's just that you'll be buying Puts instead of Calls. Two legs are a part of the trade.

The Short Put leg is placed at a strike price beyond a support level that is medium in strength. It will have an expiry date beyond 30 days but less than the second Long Put leg's expiry date. The Long Put will have the same strike price as the Short Put.

The idea is to capture the benefits of short-term neutral behavior and long-term bearishness. The Shorter Term Put provides a premium, and the Long Term Put provides capital gains in intrinsic value increases as prices dive. It is also a net debit trade.

Much like the Call Calendar Spread, the Put Spread can be adjusted depending on the type of market behavior observed. The most common adjustment methods involve converting it into a Vertical Spread to take advantage of price behavior.

This concludes our look at Horizontal Spread trades. As you can see, they're not very complex and are far easier to maintain and understand than Vertical Spread trades. Spread trades are a step up from Collars, and, like the Collar, they offer decent and steady rewards when executed correctly.

CHAPTER 5:

Rolling and Managing Option Positions

Sometimes, as a trader, you want to make adjustments to your positions and trades. You make these changes and adjustments when you notice changes in the market that will affect your trades but had not been predicted. There are several ways of managing trades, and one of these methods is known as rolling positions.

Rolling Positions

There are three basic ways of rolling options positions. You can roll forward, roll down, or even roll up a position depending on your goals. The term "roll an option" is derived from the phrase "roll down an option until it is at a lower strike price." Traders will, from time to time, need to make changes or adjustments to an existing position.

Anytime a trader closes an existing position and immediately opens a similar position with a similar number of contracts. Still, at lower strike prices, we consider this to be a roll-down process. As a trader, learning the art of rolling down a position could be crucial to your strategies and determine your performance and profitability.

Rolling Down a Position

It is possible to manage both short and long positions using rolling techniques. The same is true for both Put and Call options. When it comes to Call options, the rolling technique will send the option more into the money. However, with Put options, rolling tends to send them more out-of-the-money.

When you are holding a long position in the market, you need to create a similar order: a sell to close. You can expect to fill out an order form with your broker actually to perform a roll-on procedure. Some of the orders would require you to include a BTO, buy to open, an STC, or sell to close a position.

Purposes of Rolling Down Options

There are reasons why traders often roll down positions they hold in options Spreads. The first is to avoid assignments. When a trader rolls down a Short Put option, the main aim is to prevent any in-the-money options assigned. A trader dealing in Naked Put writing is often an extremely dangerous approach reserved only for experienced traders. Therefore, in one case, a trader will roll out a position to avoid assignment.

In other situations, a trader will roll a position to make adjustments that improve its outlook. They do so first when they wish to collect profits on a long position, especially one that is too deep in-the-money. In this instance, they will be rolled down to positions that are too deep in-the-money.

Traders also enact roll-down positions to stop a loss. When traders hold Long Call options that begin to lose money, then it is wise to roll those positions and make adjustments to stop the loss, making money instead. It is also advisable to use rolling techniques to salvage some value that is still left in a losing money position.

Rolling the Iron Condor

There are some opportunities that traders have, and one of these is rolling positions. We roll out certain positions to allow time for correction. For instance, should you be holding a position in the market that is not generating profits as it nears expiration, then you can roll this position so that it expires an extra month later. It can happen with a Naked Short Put, a Short Straddle, or a Short Strangle.

Rolling is also available to more complex positions, such as the Short Iron Condor. A Short Iron Condor is generally a short premium trade whose risk is clearly defined. However, it is a lot more difficult to roll these positions compared to more straightforward ones.

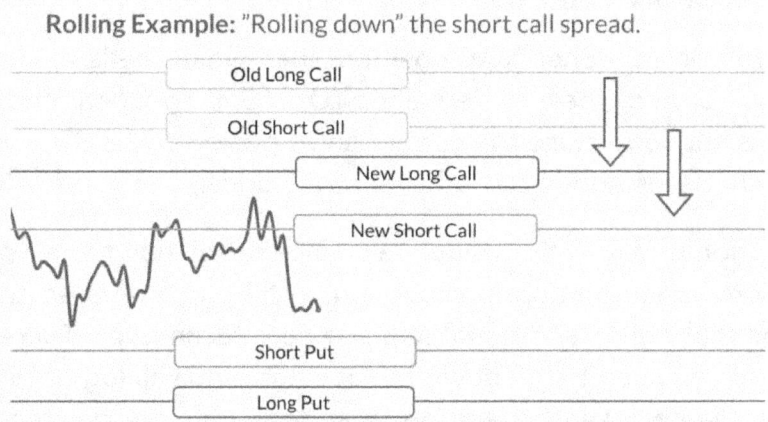

Rolling Example: "Rolling down" the short call spread.

When you roll down the Iron Condor, you may want to begin with the Short Call Spread. Do this, especially when the underlying stock price begins to fall and is heading towards the Short Put Spread. Ideally, a short Condor position often begins with no risk regarding exposure as the Delta position is zero.

However, as the trade begins to take shape, the stock price will quickly become bearish and, in the process, begin to approach the strike price of the Short Put. In this situation, the position Delta will grow, indicating that the trade is generally bullish in terms of its direction.

One of the best ways to adjust the Iron Condor is to purchase the old Call Spread to close the trade. It is the best approach to roll down the Short Call Spread. Then we will also sell a new Call option with a lower strike price. It will open another desirable trade.

Accomplishments of the Iron Condor Adjustment

When you perform this rolling process on the Iron Condor Spread, you will collect more premiums. It happens because there is a net credit that results from Call options with a higher strike price. Such options are generally cheaper and will result in a net credit.

You will also be able to stop and possibly neutralize the directional exposure that the Iron Condor would expose you to. When you roll down the Call option, then the Iron Condor will gain positive Delta. Hence, rolling ensures that the direct exposure changes direction from one that is bearish to bullish and closer to a neutral position.

Rolling Down a Short Call Position

If you want to roll down a Short Call position, then what needs to occur is to create two simultaneous orders. These orders are STO or Sell To Open, and BTC or Buy To Close. The BTC is set up to close the current short position. The STO will then be used to open a new short position but at a lower strike price.

As it is, most option brokers offer traders a chance to roll down their positions. Direct roll downs on brokerage platforms allow you to fill out orders so that you can roll down a position that needs additional management techniques. Therefore, when you finally decide that you need to roll down the position, you will log onto your brokerage platform, fill out the necessary rolling forms, and roll out your desired position.

Example: Rolling Down a Short Call Position

The shares of ABC Company are trading on the markets at $50. You have Call options in the market with a $50 strike price and hoping that there will be a short pullback. A couple of days later, ABC shares drop to $45, so you hope for a further price drop. As such, you opt to roll down the Call options that you own to a new price of $45 rather than the initial price of $50.

By rolling down the option, you will position yourself for further profits should the stock price continue to drop. By successfully lowering your strike price from $50 to $45, you will have, in essence, rolled down your position and positioned yourself to earn more money.

Rolling Down a Short Put Position

Rolling down a Put position is very close to rolling down a short position. Such an options management technique is a bearish strategy. The procedure is essentially the same. As a trader, you will execute both legs simultaneously to minimize the chances of slippage. Slippage in this instance refers to the erosion of profit, which happens where the underlying security's price changes.

When rolling a Put option, the new position will be cheaper as the strike price will be lower. The new contracts will cost less compared to the old ones. Even then, the result could end up being credit or a debit to an account. The price difference will determine how much credit or debit this will be to an account.

Reasons for Rolling Down a Short Put

There are many reasons why you would roll down a position. One of these is to prevent the exercise of an options contract by a buyer. Put buyers reserve the right to buy the underlying stock at the stated price, so if you have a Naked Put, you could end up seriously exposed.

Another reason why Put options are rolled down or managed could be to increase the bearish stand of an option with a long market position. A Long Put in-the-money will lose value, hence the need to perform a rolling procedure. By rolling out a position, traders get the opportunity to recoup any losses and receive a lot more profits for their positions in the market.

Holding a Long Call position in the market can lower the strike price if the position is rolled, especially when the underlying security loses value even if the trader has a bullish outlook on the price. As such, the position will continue to be in place after a rollout and any possible losses eliminated.

Example of Rolling a Short Put Position

The shares of ABC are trading at $50 in the market, and so, you decide to write a Short Put option at a strike price of $50. Your outlook is bullish on this position to ensure that you profit should the price go up. However, the price falls to $45, resulting in losses in some of your options. The option itself is in-the-money, so you now think it will rally back with time. To benefit from the expected upward trajectory in the underlying stock price, you will have to roll down this position.

Rolling a Short Straddle

A Short Straddle is among the most profitable strategies available in the market today. However, traders need to adjust their positions based on market needs and outlook from time to time. It is a technique that should only be left to experienced and advanced traders. Sometimes, intermediate and other traders think that adjusting a position is challenging and a complex affair. It is not the case because it is possible to make adjustments to most positions in the market. A Short Straddle is sometimes created as part of an Iron Butterfly. It involves the sale of an option at-the-money and consists of Put and a Call option. Let us take a look at an example.

Example

In our case, we have the stock ABC that trades at $20 per share. As such, we have a Call option with a strike price of $20 and a Put option with a strike price of $20. Now, both the Call and Put options are very close to being at-the-money. When this trade is converted into a Butterfly, it becomes slightly different as we purchase Call options at $25 and then sell options at $15. In this instance, we are essentially buying options at $5, so we end up with a risk-free position. Now, the initial trade at the onset has a $2 credit. If this holds, then the break-even point will lie between the strike prices of $18 and $22. We are also hoping that the trade heads in this direction. To invert this trade, we need to do it within the final 3 to four weeks before expiration. As we near expiration, we make adjustments and roll our positions to reduce risks and avert any looming losses. In this case, when the market rallies against our position and the stock rise to $23, then we will need to roll this position.

Ways of Rolling and Managing Straddle Positions

The Straddle is sometimes thought to be a rather risky strategy. However, the risks are not as bad as they are made out to be. If you are an experienced trader or perhaps an intermediate, then you can learn how to manage the position and avoid any risks and dangers that this strategy poses.

This strategy is not as risky or challenging as some may want you to believe. Here are a couple of ways of reducing risks and managing the position appropriately. Here are some circumstances you need to ensure to manage your Straddle position.

1. *Have a seriously rich premium:* It is a fact that the best and most effective Short Straddles have a very rich premium, especially when the positions are near the money or at-the-money.

2. *Positions to expire within a month.* As a trader, you need to create positions to suit your position. As such, you should ensure to close a position as soon as possible. Therefore, you need to keep a close eye on the prices. These include strike prices and current prices.

   Any slight movement in the price affects other variables such as the time factor. Therefore, should there be any unfavorable moves, we can counter these by closing at a profit.

3. *You should close positions on both sides once time decay begins:* Both sides should also be closed as soon as possible when the intrinsic value should roll the position and repeat it.

   When you roll forward your position, which might become necessary, you will save your position and duplicate it later. It might be needed on one side only, perhaps because of the factors such as time decay or price movement.

4. *Cover a Short Call:* In some situations, you may need to cover the short Put or Call should the situation Call for it. To achieve this, you will need to use either long options or stocks, even though the long options are costly.

5. *If it is profitable, then get exercised:* Sometimes, exercise can be a beneficial option, especially if it earns you a profit. What you need to ensure is that the market value of your position is profitable.

Rolling a Calendar Spread

If you have a Calendar Spread, sometimes during the trade, changes could prompt you to roll the position. You need to consider certain factors if you are to make changes as the position approaches expiration. Let us take the instance where we have a Calendar Spread in ABC trading the markets at $50. The option is currently at-the-money. This position is created by selling a nearer-term 50 Call and purchasing a deferred month 50 Call. A couple of weeks later, the Spread may not be faring as well as it was predicted. As the position approaches expiration, there is a strong desire to make certain changes or adjustments.

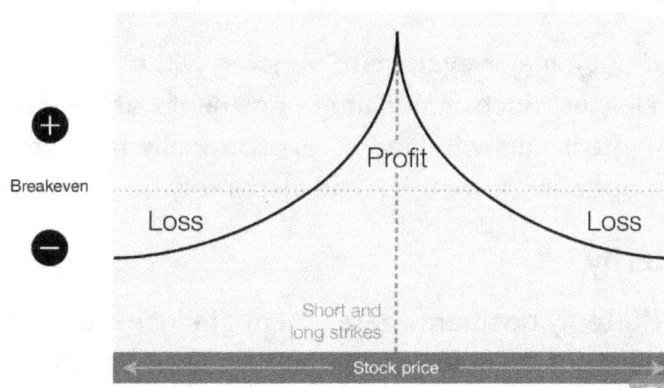

FIGURE 1: CALENDAR OPTION SPREAD PROFIT/LOSS.

Rolling the Position

There are a couple of options available to you at this stage. One of them is liquidating the Spread through the closure of the two legs. However, this is sometimes not the most advisable approach. Instead, you may want to roll the position to allow it to perform better at the markets. Rolling in this case refers to moving or adjusting an option from its current position to another one.

When rolling the calendar, we could change its strike price, its expiration date, and sometimes even both of them. Let us assume that the Short Calendar Spread is close to expiration. In this case, you can easily adjust the expiration date to a future one. You will maintain the same strike price but push the expiration date by about one month.

When you do this, you should ensure that the new expiration date is not further out in time compared to the long option. The reason is that you benefit from positive Theta. Near-term options experience a faster rate of decay compared to other options like the longer-term options.

Choosing You Strike

Generally, there are no rules or regulations regarding the expiration dates for your position after rolling. However, you will find some tradeoffs, just like all other positions, exactly how Theta plays out. You can choose to roll the position to the next eight days and, if necessary, do the same in the coming week. It is possible as long as the date does not extend beyond the necessary time to shut down the Spread position. There are a couple of other things that you may want to consider. For instance, how far out is the value of the underlying stock at this stage from the strike price? Keep in mind that changes to the strike price will have a direct impact on price expectations.

You should also find out if major events are pending within the lifetime of your options, such as earnings releases. Such major announcements often have a major effect on implied volatility. In effect, this will lead to exceptionally high stock prices, especially affecting short-term options. However, it can also imply that there is a price fluctuation.

Rolling Iron Butterfly

If you have an Iron Butterfly position where you might lose money, you would be better off rolling it rather than closing it and losing money. You can easily size up the position.

It is better to adjust the position in the direction of the market. It would be best to roll up the Iron Butterfly, and specifically the Long Put options. These should be rolled up to a higher strike price. There will be a tiny debit concerning the initial credit. The inherent risk of the strategy will decrease and Put it in a better position.

CHAPTER 6:

Getting into the Mindset of an Option Trader

Having the correct attitude is so significant if you need to be a fruitful merchant. It can be a distinct advantage. As I previously let you know, options are among the most flexible instruments in the budgetary world. You need to figure out how you can utilize them to your advantage, and one of the abilities you need to learn in the process is how you can gain the outlook of an alternatives broker.

Strategies to Think Like an Option Trader

Let me educate you regarding somewhat a mystery, which isn't a very great mystery. Suppose you genuinely need to turn into a fruitful broker. In that case, you ought not exclusively to be exceeding expectations at making sense of the best systems, yet you ought to likewise be having a triumphant outlook. A broad examination can help you get your realities straight; however, your outlook can assume a tremendous job when you are exchanging. It isn't the exchanging methodologies, immaculate market examination, or straightforward intelligence that causes you to win trading; however, it is your mental attitude that will get you far.

The vast majority of the tenderfoots I have collaborated with have consistently disclosed to me something very similar—they are attempting to make sense of the correct procedure. They, for the most part, remain very worried about doing as such. Most amateurs imagine that you should apply it, and cash will come racing into your financial balance once you have the best technique. However, that is not what occurs.

When you are in the trading scene for a long time, you will comprehend that exchanging isn't about methodologies and numbers, and some of the time, it can even be intense. There are such a large number of merchants simply like you who are sitting tight for their brilliant chance to turn into a mogul, and they are, for the most part, smart and very much educated. They even have planned full-confirmation methodologies, which are question strong. Be that as it may, you will see that even they end up losing cash every once in a while.

Then again, some merchants can show you a record of predictable successes, and do you know the mystery behind their consistency? It is their mental outlook. Exchanging brain research is a thing, in all honesty, and it is intensely inquired about. A few mental attributes, outlooks, perspectives, and convictions are concentrated under that framework. You need to know them, and on the off chance, you need to become wildly successful in the exchanging scene.

The absolute most normal convictions and mentalities about the market incorporate your feeling that the market is fixed against you. However, that is just a deception that you need to let go of. It is wrong and can place you in a negative perspective. If you continue thinking that way, you won't have the option to effectively pull off your exchanges. Nobody in the market is attempting to go against your good faith, and if you suspect as much, at that point, you need to change your viewpoint and take a gander at it in an alternate manner. If you keep on digging yourself in such unmerited considerations, you won't have the option to make the correct assessment of the open doors that emerge in the market. Recollect one thing plainly—the market isn't one-sided in any way. It is totally unbiased, and there isn't a sliver of uncertainty about that. The market couldn't care less whether you are losing all your cash or you're winning.

Your trading brain research is liable for the convictions that you have, and these convictions can get so profoundly established in your subliminal that occasionally they can drive you into a harmful pattern of self-questioning. In the following segment, we will talk about a portion of the attributes an alternative dealer ought to have to be effective, and there, you will discover that certainty is, actually, one of the most significant characteristics that you ought to have.

If you investigate the mindsets of merchants who have lost progressively, you will see that one thing is basic with a large portion of them, and that is—there is this bothering self-question that gathers all the pessimism in life. You need to understand that you are strolling in the way of an inevitable outcome on the off chance that you believe that you have misfortune; thus, you can't win. You will experience issues in starting trades at the ideal time or executing procedures at the perfect time on the off chance that you question your capacities. You won't have the option to accept the Call when you should. It can diminish your benefits as well as make a negative salary.

Then again, winning traders don't think that way. They realize how to regard the states of the market, and they realize that occasionally, their procedures can fail, or regardless of whether they did everything right, the exchange can fail. They don't fall into a pointless pattern of self-pity. They are certain about themselves and the choices they make. It certainly isolates them from losing traders, and they never lose a veritable chance coming towards them.

Something else steady with winning traders is knowing when an exchange is losing them cash and just a 'terrible exchange.' You may confound them both to be very much the same thing; however, they are certainly not. There is a basic contrast, and I will disclose that distinction to you at this moment. Your exchange can't be named an awful exchange since you lost some cash on it. That exchange is essentially losing. The arrangement of exchange to be fortunate or unfortunate isn't decided based on whether you won it or lost it, yet what makes a difference is that the potential prize is more when contrasted with the hazard. Additionally, paying little heed to how the exchange ends will be a decent exchange if the probabilities or chances support yourself. In this way, when you have taken a trade, on the off chance that you are overseeing admirably with it regardless of whether you win or lose cash, it will, in any case, be a decent exchange.

Likewise, suppose we are thinking about the opposite, regardless of whether you won cash from the exchange; however, the hazard with remunerate proportion was terrible, or if it was not started on great standing, at that point regardless of how much benefit you made. In that case, that exchange will, in any case, be viewed as awful.

Trading is a serious, demanding task, and numerous individuals neglect to comprehend that before hopping directly into it. At the point when you have a foreordained course set in your psyche, and the exchange doesn't go your direction, you will confront a horde of feelings, and the equivalent applies to the situation when the exchange goes toward you. What's more, trades frequently face an adrenaline surge along these lines, which prompts an undermining, dangerous, and upsetting circumstance. Regardless of how you are a major part of your life without a care in the world, when you enter the exchanging floor, keeping up that equivalent aura is a significant extreme errand. The pressure and the weight that you will encounter is something that you haven't previously would be intense.

To behave like an options trader, you need to figure out how to think in probabilities. Indeed, when your well-deserved cash is on the line, it may be somewhat hard to think along these lines, yet you essentially need to learn it. Let us state that a specific methodology says that when applied to a lot of exchanges, it will give you a 50-50 proportion of win/lose. All in all, in any event, when you have this information close by and have a full verification of the risks alongside an exchanging plan hand, what else would you be able to do? Nothing, since you need to follow your exchanging plan.

To put it this way, try not to feel excessively cheerful on a triumphant exchange, neither excessively discouraged on a losing one. To be an effective options trader, you need to understand that your exchanges will play out just half of the time. If you consider anybody exchanges from the various exchanges you did, that one exchange is just a little piece of the fantastic plan. It will require some investment to keep up this demeanor and thinking; however, you need to keep at it, and at exactly that point, you will have the option to build up the truckloads of control you need to be an effective options trader.

Important Traits of a Successful Options Trader

If you are thinking about what attributes of an options trader make him/her fruitful, we will talk about that in this area. There is an explanation that a few traders can beat others, and once you find out about these qualities, I trust you will be attempting to teach those in yourself.

Ability to Manage Risk

You will most likely hear everybody state repeatedly that risk management is what you need to be effective. Furthermore, traders will have the option to utilize the risk management techniques because they are not precise with chance appraisal in any case. Remembering the factor of instability, you need to comprehend what an express or verifiable position is. You likewise need to evaluate what the significant drawback of exchange can be. These are just a couple of inquiries that you ought to present yourself. When the risk is made sense, you need to be ready to discover a route to moderate the risk or control it. For instance, on the off chance that you are more into transient trades in the universe of alternatives, there will be many misfortune exchanges that you will go over in a day. Let's say you chose to hold your position for the time being, and on that equivalent night, some unfriendly news was discharged, which altered the course of the market; thus, your wager turns sour. In any case, your risk management system ought to be acceptable to the point that it can control the risk regardless of the circumstance. Enhancement is only one of the procedures that traders use to limit the dangers engaged with the trade; thus, their trade size is diminished. Another attribute that you ought to have to be a fruitful options trader is to be acceptable at overseeing cash. Regardless of how much capital you have, on the off chance that you don't oversee it admirably, it is, at last, going to go down the channel. One of the extremely normal models that I can give you is—assume a trader utilized 90% of his capital on a solitary exchange and the exchange reverse discharges to lose practically the entirety of his cash.

Have Discipline

Having a legitimate order will get you far in your options trading vocation. Be that as it may, what does mean being disciplined? It implies that you have played out an adequate measure of research, effectively distinguished the open doors in the market that can work in support of yourself, set up an exchange the correct way, structure objectives, utilize the correct methodology, and have a way-out system. Do you know when you don't have discipline? It is when you don't work on anything of your own; however, you just follow the crowd. Regardless of whether somebody gives you a tip, try not to be confident in it if you haven't played out your examination. At the point when you acquire a misfortune, it's on you and not on the individual who gave you a tip; in such a case that you had played out your examination, you would have distinguished what wasn't right with the tip. That is the reason why having a free system is so significant for everybody. A few traders have finished training in this field, yet there are likewise such many effective traders who didn't read about options trading and are as yet becoming famous. In this way, your call is whether you need to seek after your degree or not; however, to pay little heed to that, having an exhaustive thought regarding how the market functions is significant for everybody. On the off chance that you do a Google search on the most proficient method to bring in enormous cash in options trading and imagine that you have gotten the hang of everything, at that point, you are wrong. You need to delve into the subtleties and pick up everything to think about the market and its activities.

Ability to Control Emotions

Controlling your feelings is a significant piece of trading brain research. Controlling your feelings doesn't possibly apply to times when everything is awful; however, it likewise applies to the great occasions whenever you may have higher odds of committing errors since you are so excited for your success. If you ask most of the amateurs in the market, they will all reveal to you something very similar; they had made more misfortunes when they were excited and upbeat in view of success. Regardless of what number of series of wins you have, you need to remain grounded and not become presumptuous.

On the off chance that any of your exchanges end up being incorrect, you need to concede the issue and afterward pull out. Never let yourself get excessively connected to a specific stock; or, it will demolish you. Adhere to the standards you made first and foremost, and don't redirect from your way since you are passionate.

Be an Active Learner

It has been said by the CBOT or the Chicago Board of Trade that out of each individual who is trading, 90% of them are going to fail. However, the significant thing here is to gain from the misfortunes and mix-ups you have made instead of remaining ignorant about it. Practice and more practice will assist you with advancing beyond others, and for that, you have to comprehend why those misfortunes occurred so you can amend your exchange from the following exchange onwards. The market is rarely stale and is continuously advancing. You need to develop with it as well, by being a functioning student.

Keep a Record of Your Trades

Effective merchants have the propensity for recording their exchanges in a diary or another place. Do you know why? So that at whatever point a comparative circumstance emerges, later on, you recall what you did, and perhaps you can apply the system once more. Every one of your exchanges that have been finished has an abundance of data, particularly if you can remember it and use it in your trades. It will place all the chances in support of yourself.

How to Determine the Right Time to Buy or Sell?

Significantly, you purchase or sell your options at the correct time; else, you probably won't have the chance to bring home good profits. In this way, here are a few variables to remember that will assist you with settling on your choice.

Is the Option Underpriced or Overpriced?

I comprehend what you should think—you are thinking about how you might discover whether an option is overrated or undervalued. To find that, you need to figure what its natural worth is. It is not the same as how you do it on account of values, and the model followed on account of choices is known as the Black and Scholes model. With this model, you will have the option to discover the inborn worth. I am not delving into the equation's insights because you will get it there once you go to your trading stage.

You have to comprehend that an option will be classified as overrated when its cost is more than the characteristic worth, and such options must be sold. In actuality, an option will be ordered as undervalued if its cost is not exactly the characteristic worth, and such a choice must be a branch.

Check the Volatility

When you are attempting to see if you should purchase alternatives or sell them, unpredictability assumes a major job, and you will perceive how. Unpredictability is one such factor that can profit both Put and Call options. On the upside, the alternative turns out to be considerably more significant, and on the drawback, there is a restricted hazard.

In more straightforward terms, if instability builds, the estimation of alternative increments excessively independent of how the stock's cost is at a similar point. In this way, when such an occasion happens, you need to purchase options and sell the options when you notice a reduction in unpredictability.

The occurrence of Major Events

It is constantly encouraged that before any significant occasions happen or before any geopolitical issue emerges, you ought not to sell your options and rather get them. Envision what might have occurred if, before the Greek emergency, you had sold your Put options. If you purchase the options instead of selling, all you will lose is the premium paid. Be that as it may, on the off chance that you decide to sell them, at that point, there is a risk of your whole capital being cleared out.

Are You Taking a Defensive View or an Affirmative One?

Your choice to sell or purchase an option will be significantly affected by your view on the record or stock. Let me clarify the importance of the two perspectives with the goal that we are clear. At the point when you believe that a specific stock is going to go down or definitively going up conclusively, that is the point at which you have an agreed view. On the chance that your view is certifiable, contingent on the case, you can either purchase a Put option or a Call option. Be that as it may, then again, on the off chance that you have a protective view, at this point, you ought to sell the option. For instance, imagine that a specific stock A won't ascend above $10, at that point, it would be a superior option that you sell your $12 Call option on this stock as opposed to purchasing.

Expiration Date

The termination date or the time left to expiry is a significant factor of options that assumes a job in nearly everything. Like I previously let you know, in contrast to stocks, there is a fixed date of expiry for each option agreement before which it must be worked out; else, it will get pointless. In any case, this factor of time works in the kindness of vendors and against purchasers. The time rot is very steady at the outset; however, as the time and the expiry date begin diminishing, the rot happens quicker. In easier terms, the estimation of the option declines quicker. Things being what they are, when options are near their lapse date, it's anything but a smart thought to get them, right?

It is a vital choice regarding whether you need to purchase options or sell them, yet you need to consider it thoroughly whatever choice you make.

CHAPTER 7:

How to Maximize Profits with Options Trading

Now it is time to move on to some of the steps you can take to maximize your profits with options. Options are a great way to earn a profit because they allow you to reduce your exposure and the amount of risk you take on while increasing the number of profits you could make. Some of the tips that you can use to help maximize your profits while options trading includes:

Tip 1: You Can Profit no Matter the Market Situation

One of the first things that you will notice when working in the options market is that you can benefit from any situation in the market when you work with options. Most of the strategies that work with this investment vehicle are carried out by combining the different option positions. Sometimes, they will even use the underlying position of the stock. You can use different trading strategies or work with a few to profit no matter what market situation.

When you enter the market with options, you always stand to make huge profits while still keeping your risk to a minimum. Ordinary stock trading isn't as reliable, and it comes with a lot more risk. The most crucial aspects of options trading are when you should enter a trade and exit it. Knowing how and when to exit will ensure that you keep any losses to a minimum and that you can increase your profits as much as possible.

You will find that options strategies are considered one of the most versatile in the financial market. They will provide investors and traders alike with many profit-making opportunities, and there is a limited amount of risk and exposure present. It is one of the main reasons that many investors like to take some time and invest in options instead of other asset choices.

Since you can profit no matter what the market situation is doing, It gives you a lot of freedom when working with options. But it also means that you may have to learn a lot more strategies than usual. You should learn at least a few strategies for a rising market, a stagnant market, and a downturn market. It will ensure that you are ready to go no matter which way the market is heading.

While making a profit in any market is a great thing and can open up many new opportunities to make money compared to just investing in the stock market, it does make things a bit trickier to work with. You have to understand where the market is going, you have to know which strategies work for the different market directions, and you have to be ready to switch back and forth depending on how the market is doing.

Tip 2: Take Advantage of The Volatility of Options to Make A Profit

Options have some similarities to stocks, but they are a bit different and one place you will notice these differences is with the time limit. Stocks can be held for as short of a period or as long as you want, but options have an expiration date. It means that the time you get to make the trade is going to be limited. And as a trader, missing this window will be a costly mistake, one that you need to avoid if at all possible. If this chance is missed, then it may be a very long time before you see it again.

It is why it is never a good idea to work with a long-term strategy when you are trying to trade with options. Strategies, such as working with the average down, are seen as bad choices for options trading because you simply don't get the right time frame to see them happen. Also, make sure that you are careful about margin requirements. Depending on what these are, they could have a big impact on the requirements for the number of funds you can invest.

There are also times when multiple factors may affect a favorable price. For instance, the price of the asset you choose may go up, which is usually seen as a good thing. But it is possible that any of the accruing benefits could be eroded due to other factors, such as volatility, time decay, and dividend payment. These constraints mean that you need to learn how to follow some of the Different Strategies for Profit-Taking.

Tip 3: Always Set A Profit-Taking Stop Loss

The next tip that you should follow is to set up a profit-taking stop loss. You can set up a stop loss at about five percent. It means that you want it to reach a target price of $100 if the trailing target is $95. If the upward trend continues and the price gets to $120, then the trailing target, assuming the 5 percent from before, will become $114. And it would keep going up from there, with the amount of profit you wish to make in the process.

Now, let's say that the price is going to start to fall. When this happens, you will need to exit and then collect the profits at this level or the trailing target you set. It ensures that you get to enjoy some protection as the price increases, and then you will exit the trade as soon as the price starts to turn around. The thing that you need to remember here is that the stop loss levels should never be too high or too low. If they are too small, you will be kicked out of the market too soon in most cases. But if they are too high, they will make it impossible to enjoy profit-taking.

Tip 4: Sell Covered Call Options Against Long Positions

Selling options is an income-generating process that is pretty lucrative. Depending on the amount of risk you take and what kinds of trades you decide to do, you could easily take home more than two percent in returns each month. However, this is not the only method you can use to make it rich on the market. You can also go with something that is known as a Naked Put and sell these. It is similar in the way of selling stocks or shares that you don't own.

When you sell a Naked Put option, you will be able to free up some of your time to do more. Stock trading allows you to have an opportunity to sell stocks of shares that you don't already own, and then you can earn a profit. It will free up your capital, allowing you to invest it or trade with it indefinitely.

To let this method work, it's best to deal with stocks that you already understand well or those you wouldn't mind owning. This way, you know when there are any major changes to the stock, and you can make some changes to the way you invest before the market turns and harms your profits. There is still a level of hedging associated with this options trading method, so you must always be on the lookout for that.

Tip 5: Pick the Right Strategy

Often, the one that you pick will lead you to find the right options to sell. Some of the options trading strategies are going to work in a downturn, some are going to work the best in an upturn, and some do well when the market is more stagnant. When you pick out a strategy, you will choose the options that fit in with that strategy the best.

With that said, there are a few guidelines that you can learn to follow when it is time to purchase an option for trading. Following these guidelines will make it easier for you to identify the options you should choose to profit from. Some of the guidelines include:

- Determine whether the market is bullish or bearish. Also, make sure that you determine whether you are strongly bullish or just mildly bullish. It can make a difference in how the market is doing and which assets you would like to work with.

- Think about how volatile the market is right now and how it could affect your strategy with options trading. Also, you can think about the status of the market at the time. Is the market currently calm, or is there a lot of volatility that shows up? If it is not very high, you should be able to buy the Call options based on the underlying stock, and these are usually seen as relatively inexpensive.

- Consider the strike price and the expiration date of any options you want to trade-in. If you only have a few shares at this time, this may make it the best time to purchase more of the stock or asset.

- Your overall goal of working with the options trading market is to make as much profit as possible. No one goes into the market, or any kind of investment, with the idea that they want to lose money. But if you follow some of the tips above, you will maximize your profits and see some great results.

CHAPTER 8:

Financial Leverage from Experts

While it should come as no surprise that you are going to need to gather as much data as possible to make the best trades, regardless of what market you are working in; it is important to keep in mind that if you don't use it in the right way, then it is all for naught. There are two ways to get the most out of any of the data you gather; the first is via technical analysis, and the second is via fundamental analysis. As a general rule, you will likely find it helpful to start with fundamental analysis before moving on to technical analysis as the need arises. To understand the difference between the two, you may find it helpful to think about technical analysis as analyzing charts. In contrast, fundamental analysis looks at specific factors based on the underlying asset for the market that you are working in. The core tenant of fundamental analysis is that related details can tell the whole story regarding the market in question.

In contrast, technical analysis believes that the only required details relate to the price at the moment. As such, fundamental analysis is typically considered easier to master than concepts less expressly related to understanding market movement exclusively. Meanwhile, technical analysis is typically faster because key fundamental analysis data is often only publicly available on a strict and limited schedule. Sometimes only a few times a year, meaning the availability for updating specific data is rather limited.

Fundamental Analysis Rules

The best time to use fundamental analysis is when you are looking to gain a broad idea of the state of the market as it stands and how that relates to the state of things shortly when it comes time to trading successfully. Regardless of what market you are considering, the end goals are the same, find the most effective trade for the time you are targeting. Establish a baseline: to begin analyzing the fundamentals, the first thing that you will need to do is create a baseline regarding the company's overall performance. To generate the most useful results possible, the first thing you will need to do is gather data regarding the company in question and the related industry as a whole. When gathering macro data, it is important to keep in mind that no market will operate in a vacuum, which means the reasons behind specific market movement can be much more far-reaching than they first appear. Fundamental analysis works because of the stock market's propensity for patterns, which means if you trace a specific market moved back to the source, you will have a better idea of what to keep an eye on in the future.

Furthermore, all industries go through several different phases where their penny stocks will be worth more or less overall based on general popularity. If the industry is producing many popular penny stocks, then overall volatility will be down while at the same time liquidity will be at an overall high. Consider worldwide issues: once you have a general grasp on the current phase you are dealing with, the next thing you will want to consider is anything that is going on in the wider world that will after the type of businesses you tend to favor in your penny stocks. Not being prepared for major paradigm shifts, especially in penny stocks where new companies come and go so quickly, means that you can easily miss out on massive profits and should be avoided at all costs. To ensure you are not blindsided by news you could have seen coming, it is important to look beyond the obvious issues that are consuming the 24-hour news cycle and dig deeper into the comings and goings of the nations going to most directly affect your particular subsection of penny stocks. One important worldwide phenomenon that you will want to pay specific attention to is anything in technology. Major paradigm shifts like smartphones' adoption or electric cars' current move can create serious paradigm shifts.

Put it all together

Once you have a clear idea of what the market should look like and what may be on the horizon, the next step is to put it all together to compare what has been and what might the current state of the market be. It will give you a realistic idea of what other investors will do if certain events occur the way they have in the past. Furthermore, you will be able to use these details to identify underlying assets currently on the cusp of generating the type of movement you need if you want to utilize them via binary options trading. The best time to get on board with a new underlying asset is when it is nearing the end of the post-bust period or the end of a post-boom period depending on if you are going to place a Call or a Put. In these scenarios, you will have the greatest access to the market's freedom and thus have access to the greatest overall allowable risk you will find in any market. Remember, the amount of risk that you can successfully handle without an increase in the likelihood of failure is going to start decreasing as soon as the boom or bust phase begins in earnest, so it is important to get in as quickly as possible if you hope to maximize your profits truly. Understand the relative strength of any given trade. When an underlying asset is experiencing a boom phase, the strength of its related fundamentals will determine how other investors will act when it comes to binary options trading. Keeping this in mind, it then stands to reason that the earlier a given underlying asset is in a particular boom phase, the stronger the market surrounding it will be. Remember, what an underlying asset looks like isn't nearly as important as what it is likely to look like in the future when it comes to fundamental analysis. The best way to determine those details is by keeping an eye on the past.

Quantitative Fundamental Analysis

The sheer volume of data and a large number of varying numbers found in the average company's financial statements can easily be intimidating and bewildering for conscientious investors who are digging into them for the first time. Once you get the hang of them, however, you will quickly find that they are a goldmine of information when determining how likely a company is to continue producing reliable dividends in the future. At their most basic, a company's financial statements disclose the information relating to its financial performance over a set time. Unlike qualitative concepts, financial statements provide cold, hard facts about a rarely open company for interpretation. Important statements Balance sheet: A balance sheet shows a detailed record of all of a company's equity, liabilities, and assets for a given time. A balance sheet shows a balance to a company's financial structure by dividing its equity by combining shareholders and liabilities to determine its current assets. In this case, assets represent the resources that the company is actively in control of at a specific point in time. It can include things like buildings, machinery, inventory, cash, and more. It will also show the total value of any financing that has been used to generate those assets. Financing can come from either equity or liabilities. Liabilities include debt that must be paid back eventually, while equity, in this case, measures the total amount of money that its owners have put into the business. It can include profits from previous years, which are known collectively as retained earnings.

Income statement

While the balance sheet can be thought of as a snapshot of the company's fundamental economic aspects, an income statement takes a closer look at its performance exclusively for a given timeframe. There is no limit to the length of time an income statement considers, which means you could see them generated month to month or even day to day; however, the most common type used by public companies are either annual or quarterly. Income statements provide information on profit, expenses, and revenues that resulted from the business that took place over a specific period.

Cash flow statement

The cash flow statement frequently shows all of the cash outflow and inflow for the company over a given period. The cash flow statement often focuses on operating cash flow, which is the cash that day-to-day business operations will generate. It will also include any cash available from investing, which is often used to invest in assets, along with any cash that might have been generated by long-term asset sales or the sale of a secondary business that the company previously owned. Cash due to financing is another name for money paid off or received based on issuing or borrowing funds. The cash flow statements are quite important as it is often more difficult for businesses to manipulate them than many other types of financial documents. While accountants can manipulate earnings with ease, it is much more difficult to fake having access to cash in the bank where none exists. It is why many savvy investors consider the cash flow statement the most reliable way to measure a specific company's performance.

Finding the details

While tracking down all the disparate financial statements on the company you are considering purchasing stock in can be cumbersome, the Securities and Exchange

Commission (SEC) requires all publicly traded companies to submit regular filings outlining all of their financial activities, including a variety of different financial statements. It also includes information such as managerial discussions, reports from auditors, deep dives into the operations and prospects of upcoming years, and lot of others.

These types of details can all be found in the 10-K filing that each company is required to file every year, along with the 10-Q filing that they must send out once per quarter. Both types of documents can be found online, both at the corporate website and on the SEC website. As the version that hits the corporate site doesn't need to be complete, it is best to visit SEC.gov and get to know the Electronic Data Gathering, Analysis, and Retrieval system (EDGAR) which automates the process of indexing, validating, collecting, forward and accepting submissions. As the system was designed in the mid-90s, it is important to dedicate some time to learning the process as it is more cumbersome than 20 years of user interface advancements have lead you to expect.

Qualitative Fundamental Analysis

Qualitative factors are generally less tangible and include name recognition, the patents it holds, and its board members' quality.

Qualitative factors to consider include Business model: The first thing you will want to do when you catch wind of a company that might be worth following up on is to check out its business model, which is more or less a generalization of its making money. You can typically find these sorts of details on the company website or in its 10-K filing.

Competitive advantage

It is also important to consider the various competitive advantages that the company you have your eye on might have over its competition. Companies that will be successful in the long-term will always have an advantage over their competition in one of two ways. They can either have better operational effectiveness or improved strategic positioning. Operational effectiveness is the name given to doing the same things as the competition but more efficiently and effectively. Strategic positioning occurs when a company gains an edge by doing things that nobody else is doing.

Changes to the company

To properly narrow down your search, you will typically find the most reliable results when it comes to companies that have recently seen major changes to their corporate structure, as it is these types of changes that are likely to ultimately precede events that are more likely to see the company jump to the next level. The specifics of what happened in this instance are nearly as important as statistically speaking, 95 percent of companies that experience. This type of growth started with a significant change to the status quo.

CHAPTER 9:

Exit Strategies to Capture Profits Reliably

How many times have you turned unrealized gains into losses? If this happens to you, you may need to learn how to implement your exit strategy reliably. There is an old saying: *"Never make a profit at a loss."* this simple rule is always crucial for successful trading. Unless you always implement a reliable exit strategy, your trading success is far from what it could or should be. Your profitability is unreliable. You increase your chances of success against yourself. It can lead to a more significant loss, dissatisfaction with the trading performance, and even distrust.

Why You Need an Exit Strategy

By reliably applying your exit strategy to each trade, several of your trades will be profitable. Your winnings are usually more substantial. Over time, you become more successful. And for losing trades, your losses are generally smaller. Emotions will no longer pollute your decision, and you will never allow unrealized gains to become losses.

You need to have complete confidence in your exit strategy because if you trust my exit strategy, it is psychologically easy to automatically implement it into every transaction. You should never experience doubt, confusion, or hesitation.

Three Phases of the Transaction

Each transaction has three phases: input, knowledge, and go out. Each step has an exit strategy. Your trade will be more successful if you let the profit run, and the losses will be reduced. It means that you should always determine when your prognosis is bad before opening a position. As soon as your prediction turns out to be incorrect, close your position immediately. Leave what's left. You no longer have a reason to stay in this store. Stop-loss determines when a trade needs to be closed. I use three-loss methods, one for each phase of my trades:

- Loss of input loss, set before opening the position;

- Loss of rear brake, set if the trade moves in my favor and

- Profit stop-loss gain profit after reaching my waypoint.

Before opening my position, I always set a loss. I put it one percent below the recent strong swing on the daily stock price chart for bull trades. If the stock creates an everyday closing price during this income loss, I will leave in the morning. My prediction was wrong: stocks are falling, not going up.

If the stock rises as expected and does not stop when entering at the entry-level, I will increase the rear stop losses by one percent in the event of subsequent damages due to fluctuations. I was rattling them: while the ratchet effect reduces potential losses and blocks profits, my stops are also due to the daily closing price. The next day, each regular closing price is activated in the event of another loss of a stop.

Your Business Waypoint

You should also estimate where you reasonably expect the stock price to go. You need to decide in advance how to close your trade to maximize your profit when you reach your waypoint. Once the transaction reaches your waypoint, implement your exit strategy with strict discipline. It is not a good idea to simply end a trade when you reach your point on the route. It is better to stay in the trade as long as it continues in your favor.

However, you should leave your trading at the first sign that the market poses an unrealized risk of your unrealized profits.

When I reach my waypoints, I use much stricter termination criteria that make it easier to activate the output. After start-up, stocks are reduced rather than continued. I'll just stay in the box while stocks keep growing. Every day I move my surplus to the intraday layer. As soon as the shares are trading below yesterday's minimum, I will immediately leave. By definition, stocks fell. At this point, the population is more likely to continue to shrink than to keep.

Adjust Your Excessive Losses

The market provides a lot of advice that your unrealized profit is at increased risk of. Profit losses cease to threaten unrealized gains. You can use one or more of the following criteria to make a profit. You can stop:

- As soon as the share price turns towards you;

- As more quickly as the trend line breaks;

- As more quickly as price support is interrupted; or,

- As more quickly as a simple moving average breaks.

Each of these terms warns you that your trade is likely to start and that your unrealized gains are more likely to be at risk. If all these criteria are met: you must close the course permanently!

In addition to this standard procedure, I will be able to override other stop-loss strategies based on the pricing model, indices, options, and time. In the bear, I'm just about the process.

This way, you manage your Exits Strategy. You can make profits and reduce losses. And that should keep you from turning unrealized gains into losses.

The identification of exits falls into the trading system category; exits must be located in meaningful places on the market, determined by support and resistance. However, it is always essential to determine the initial output before starting a transaction. And then you have to leave the trade when the stop asks you to.

1. Order to lose the first stop

The first step is to get you out of the trade if the trade goes wrong at the beginning of the operation. Many systems have both a first and a rear stop, but the rear stop may not be known until certain conditions are met.

The ideal first stop should also allow for a "breathing space," but not so large that the trader can take excessive risk.

Use a strategy to stop the loss based on market price, critical levels of support, or some level of retracement.

2. Break-even stop is another common exit strategy.

Loss of clues can be shifted to the entry price when the market moves in your favor, and this is one way to secure a winning trade before using reverse cessation strategies. This method is widely used and popular because it reduces anxiety in trading.

3. Use the backstop to capture profits when the market moves in favor of traders

There are many reversal strategies to choose from. A fundamental exit strategy is two steps. The highest or lowest of the last two measures are the levels to which the trader must shift his stop loss to secure earnings. This strategy is excellent for trading within a day or when a trader expects the market to move to a consolidation sentence.

4. For emotional reasons, do not move the stop.

It is the rule, and I would like to add a comment on this topic with exit strategies because it is the number one rule to follow. Acting according to plan and sticking to plan excludes emotions. This rule ensures that exit strategies serve their purpose, and traders can reap the benefits.

5. Apply timeout

Most trading systems would terminate trade before a significant economic event, such as non-agricultural farms' payment. A time stop is used to stop trading before this reporting event to prevent market fluctuations. Market volatility risk decreases with delay.

Each time you enter a trade of any kind, you must first make sure that your exit strategy is planned, regardless of whether it ends in a winner or a loser. Knowing how to manage your trading and the right exit strategy are the most critical aspects of trading in the market.

Options trading, like any other type of trading, requires careful planning and execution. I could say every day you have some kind of participation in the market. We are all in the business. As a trader, it is easy to enter and leave the market at the touch of a button. But once you're inside, do you have a clear exit strategy?

Trading is like a business that requires planning with strategies that show you want to grow your business. In trading, a solid business plan is necessary for successful trading. Blinding in the market is just a sign that you are speculating or "rushing" to see which direction you are heading. Like all plans, you need the right approach and an even better exit strategy.

What do you do when your trade goes bad? Can you find a way to save what's left, or will you just let go when you think the market can recover? Most of us can choose the first opportunity to keep what we can and propose a strategy to save the current situation. At that point, it may be too late because all planning must take place before starting a trade. Depending on the trade, you should have a good exit strategy that complements your trading strategy and timing. In short time frames, such as 5–15 minnutes, an exit strategy must be planned before executing a trade because you do not have time to think about your termination. If you have 1 hour–4 hours, you have much more time, and you can still afford to come up with your exit strategy.

In professional trading, these "professionals" always have in mind an entry and exit strategy after analyzing market conditions and only need to follow their plan. They emphasized the balanced conduct of trade and already favored entry or exit. Both are equally important to them.

If you are like most beginners who believe that you can achieve an individual winner with all the exact entry points, I am amazed at the result. I came across several "safe winners" based precisely on entry points, but it turned out that I was a massive loss due to the inability to leave at the right time. Think about it every time you trade with a clear exit strategy.

CHAPTER 10:

Protecting Capital and Managing Money

Your mindset provides you with a strong opportunity to hedge yourself against risk in your trades, but it is not the only way to protect yourself. You also need to make sure that you are protecting yourself in practical ways against risks in the market to take advantage of all of the tools available to help you succeed.

When it comes to trading, you can never be too careful, and you should always be exercising every technique possible to protect yourself against risks in the market.

Protecting Through Diversifying

One of the best things you can do to protect yourself when you are trading is diversifying your portfolio. Diversifying your portfolio means investing your capital into multiple different trade deals to invest in several different areas. The reason why diversification hedges you against risk is that it prevents you from the likelihood of total losses.

In this case, if one of your trades does not perform well, another one of your trades is likely to outperform it and make up for that loss. As long as you are doing your best research to every single trade and trade with confidence, you are likely to see success in many of your trades if you use this strategy, and the losses you do see will not be nearly as catastrophic.

People who want to earn a serious profit with trading are virtually always investing in multiple deals at once to ensure their success, as this increases your potential for maximizing profits as well.

When it comes to diversifying, there are three ways that you can do it. The first way is to become involved in multiple trade deals that are all fairly similar, for example, getting involved in multiple different options trades.

If you are brand new to trading, you should first use this diversification style and master trading options before moving on to any other investment or trading form. This way, you can develop your confidence and skill in options first before venturing into a new trading strategy.

The other two types of diversification that you can engage in with trades include diversifying with non-correlating assets and diversifying your risk category. Both of these will help you limit your risk while also improving your money management skills, which will ultimately help you become a smart and successful trader.

Diversifying Your Risk Category

The other way that you can and should diversify your portfolio is through diversifying your risk category. When it comes to trading, there are three risk categories that you can fall into, including conservative, moderate, and high. Conservative trades allow you to guarantee a profit from your gains; however, the amount being guaranteed is often very small and does not generally have room for significant growth.

Moderate trades do carry a higher risk with them; however, they also earn you bigger profits in the long run. If you trade moderately, a strong trading strategy can help you succeed with those trades, which will increase your chances of securing your profits. High-risk category trades have a high potential to fail, but they will carry massive profits with them if they do succeed. These tend to be the most stressful investments because of how large the risk is, but the returns you get can be huge if they go through.

Generally, every trader has a risk category that they tend to stick to with most of their trades. This category will likely fluctuate as they grow older; the older you get, the more you will need to have your profits available for you to use, and the less time you will have to recover from any losses you incur in your trades. For this reason, it is advised that you use your age to help you determine what risk category you should be trading with when you are making trades.

The easiest way to determine your category is to subtract your age from 100. The value of your age should be the percentage of your funds invested into conservative investments, whereas the value remaining is free to be invested in moderate or high-risk investments. Ideally, you should further apply this rule to decide which percentage should be invested in moderate risk versus which should be invested in high risk so that your money is always being invested in an appropriate way for your age.

For example, if you are 25, then 25% of your overall investment capital should be invested in conservative investments. Then, 25% of your remaining investment capital should be invested in moderate investments, with your other 75% being invested in high-risk investments.

If you are 60, then 60% of your overall investment capital should be invested in conservative profiles, and 60% of your remaining investment capital should be invested in moderate investments. The rest can be invested in high-risk investments. You can always adapt your chosen strategy based on what you feel your needs are and what level of risk you are willing to incur, but using this as a guideline is a great way to ensure that you are managing your money properly.

This way, you can maximize your profits while also ensuring that the capital you need will be accessible when you need it at any period in your life.

Diversifying with Non-Correlating Assets

This is a strategy that you can execute almost right away when you begin trading options. The key to this diversification is that the underlying assets you are trading are different from all of your trades. For example, some of your trades may involve assets such as bonds and ETFs, whereas others might include commodities and currencies.

By changing the underlying assets that are being traded, you hedge yourself against fluctuations in the specific stock that you are investing in and the industry that this stock is a part of. In this case, if the industry itself takes a hit, you are not at risk of having every single trade deal you have made suffer due to it. Instead, you can feel confident that a substantial portion of your portfolio remains unhindered from that fluctuation, and you have no reason to panic.

If you want to take this a step further, after you have grown confident in options, you can begin to diversify your trading style by investing some of your funds elsewhere.

I will not elaborate too much on this as it is not relevant to swing trading with options; however, I understand that it can protect you in your investment portfolio overall while also giving you the greatest earning potential with your capital.

The 5% Risk Account

Some people think that a trade deal should only include the capital required to buy into that trade deal, including the cost per share and the commissions you pay to the brokerage to make your deal. While it is true that this is the only money you require to get involved in a trade, it is not true that it is the only amount that you should set aside for a trade.

If you want to manage your money effectively and hedge yourself against risk, you should always invest 5% of a total investment amount into a "risk account." This account ensures that you have enough capital to recover the losses should one occur, enabling you to carry on trading. Without it, you might find that some of your losses have catastrophic impacts on your bottom line and significantly reduce the number of trades you can afford to engage in actively, which directly damages your profitability.

Keeping that risk account open with 5% of your total investment capital (or more if you are engaging in riskier trades) will ensure that you are protected and continue to make trades even if you experience a loss.

The 2% Rule of Money Management

In addition to ensuring that your portfolio is diversified with different investments and risk categories, you also want to make sure that you manage your capital with each trade you make. Ideally, you should never be trading more than 2% of your overall investment capital into any single trade. So, if you have 5000 to invest, you should never be investing more than $100 into any given trade.

It ensures that you diversify your portfolio enough to protect yourself against risks while also increasing your likelihood of gaining profits from each trade. If you trade more than 2% of your investment capital into any given risk, you massively expose yourself to losses which can devastate your portfolio and your investments.

Realizing this rule and putting it to work in your trading portfolio might seem overwhelming early on when you are brand new to trading. You might find yourself concerned that you will not effectively manage all 50 trades, which is a reasonable fear when it comes to starting as a trader. Understand that enacting this rule does not mean that you are obligated to get started in 50 different trades all at once, effectively overwhelming yourself with attempting to manage them all.

Instead, you can start with managing just one trade, then increase to managing 3-5 trades, and then continue increasing until all of your investment capital is sunk into different investments.

Gradually increasing the number of trades you are involved with and will not only help you grow used to managing all of these trades, but it will also prevent you from becoming fearful or overwhelmed and making emotional trade deals. Early on, it is perfectly okay to start small and build your way up as your confidence grows, as this can be a powerful opportunity to increase your success in trades.

Keeping 30% of Profits

When you begin trading, you must always keep a percentage of the profits that you are earning from each trade deal. It might feel like a good idea to sink all of your profits back into your trades and profit even more, but trust me when I say this is not the best idea. Investing all of your profits back into trades can make trading feel fruitless and can work against your desire to stay committed and persistent with all your trades.

With all of the effort you are putting into making those profits happen; if you are not at least sometimes rewarding yourself by cashing out on some of them so that you can experience the tangible benefits, it might begin to feel pointless.

If you are trading to increase your capital and not as a way to replace your income, you might only want to keep 10-25% of your overall profits for yourself in your trades. This capital should be put toward fulfilling the goal outlined before you began investing, such as setting aside money to buy a house or paying off some debt. This way, you are achieving your purpose with trading while continually investing even more into your trades so that you can do even more in the future.

If you are trading intending to replace your income entirely, you want to use the right strategy to get there so that you can comfortably leave your job while still having enough to afford the cost of living. In this case, you would want to cash out about 30% of your overall profits from each trade and apply that to your cost of living.

Until you can reasonably live off of 30% of your profits, you should refrain from quitting your job so that you do not quit before you can comfortably support yourself. Ideally, you should set aside that 30% in a savings account early on so that it can quickly be accessed should you require it after you have quit your job. You should also seek to have 30% of your profits cover your cost of living for at least three months before you quit to ensure that you can consistently produce a strong enough income to keep yourself afloat after you quit your job.

You should never cash out on more than 30% of your profits from your trades when it comes to investing in the stock market. While you may want to adjust it from time to time should the need arise, you should not make a habit because it can seriously eat into your bottom line. When it comes to trading, the profits you earn are used to help you make even larger profits as they are used to hedge you against losses in other trades. If everything goes right, you end up with far more to invest, and the 30% that you cash out on increases every time. If not, that profit margin will cover any losses incurred in a bad trade deal, effectively financially protecting you from the risk.

CHAPTER 11:

Learning How to Read an Options Chart

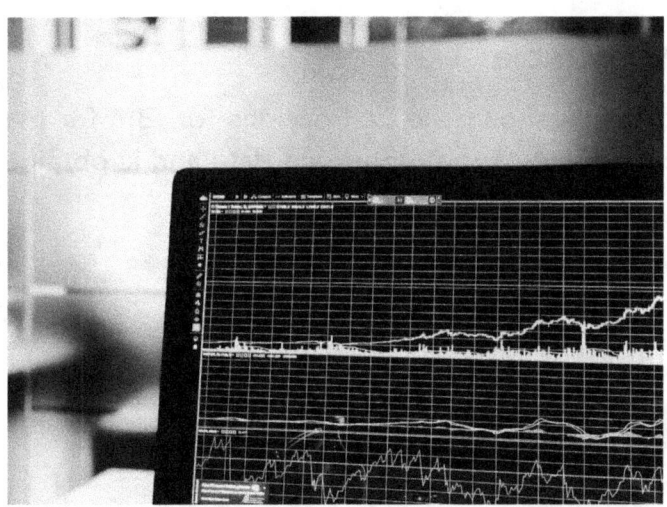

Many traders and investors have come to learn of the numerous benefits associated with options trading. Many more desire to become wealthy enough through options trading. That's why the trading volumes at options exchanges have increased steadily over the years. Data dissemination and electronic trading have enabled more traders and investors to participate in options trading. To create wealth and generate a recurrent income from trading, you must understand the trading process, terminology, and other useful features. Some investors and traders make use of options to speculate about price direction. Others use them to hedge either an anticipated or existing position, while others come up with unique positions that offer irregular benefits. Such benefits are generally unavailable to regular traders.

For instance, as an options trader, you can earn profits should an underlying stock remain unchanged. One of the crucial success factors in options trading is selecting the correct option or even a combination. These are options that are essential for the creation of a position that harbors the appropriate risk-to-reward opportunities. To be successful and create substantial wealth, you need to be a savvy trader. What you need to do at the options market is to find sophisticated data sets that will earn you attractive rewards.

Previous Era Options Trading

Back in the past decade or so, options price reports were sent to newspapers. The newspapers would list a lot of rows of data. Most of the data was illegible, and most people could not decipher its meaning. Such data was often printed in the financial sector of the newspapers. Today, however, traders are choosing to search for options data via online sources. Even when each source formats its data differently, the data and variables used are the ones found to be necessary and essential by today's traders.

Modern Day Options Table

The table indicated below shows the Call options for IBM for March. The table is a computer-generated representation of the said data and is obtained from Optionetics Platinum Software. We will examine the variables listed.

1	2	3	4	5	6	7	8	9	10	11	12
OpSym	Bid (pts)	Ask (pts)	Extrinsic Bid/Ask (pts)	IV Bid/Ask (%)	Delta Bid/Ask (%)	Gamma Bid/Ask (%)	Vega Bid/Ask (pts/% IV)	Theta Bid/Ask (pts/day)	Volume	Open Interest	Strike
IBM MAR10 110 C	16.25	16.70	0.00 / 0.37	19.77 / 35.15	99.16 / 92.06	0.27 / 1.15	0.007 / 0.053	0.0009 / -0.0279	0	479	110.000
IBM MAR10 115 C	11.65	11.80	0.32 / 0.47	25.37 / 27.68	90.52 / 88.67	1.82 / 1.90	0.060 / 0.069	-0.0227 / -0.0290	47	552	115.000
IBM MAR10 120 C	7.15	7.30	0.82 / 0.97	21.85 / 23.30	79.89 / 78.51	3.53 / 3.45	0.101 / 0.105	-0.0344 / -0.0385	360	1179	120.000
IBM MAR10 125 C	3.40	3.50	2.07 / 2.17	19.04 / 19.75	58.20 / 57.98	5.65 / 5.46	0.141 / 0.141	-0.0431 / -0.0448	1268	5782	125.000
Stock											126.33
IBM MAR10 130 C	1.10	1.14	1.10 / 1.14	17.41 / 17.73	28.66 / 29.04	5.40 / 5.33	0.123 / 0.124	-0.0349 / -0.0358	1868	5947	130.000
IBM MAR10 135 C	0.23	0.25	0.23 / 0.25	16.73 / 17.08	8.45 / 8.91	2.56 / 2.61	0.056 / 0.058	-0.0154 / -0.0164	666	6539	135.000
IBM MAR10 140 C	0.04	0.06	0.04 / 0.06	17.04 / 18.12	1.82 / 2.47	0.72 / 0.88	0.016 / 0.021	-0.0045 / -0.0062	80	4284	140.000
IBM MAR10 145 C	0.00	0.03	0.00 / 0.02	0.00 / 21.03	0.00 / 1.17	0.00 / 0.40	0.000 / 0.011	0.0000 / -0.0038	10	1747	145.000

If you can learn to read the table above, you will be on your way to understanding stock options and increasing your chance of earning big money. The columns run down while the rows run across. Let us examine the columns closely.

OPSYM

It is found in the first column. The field indicated here represents the underlying stock which in this case is IBM. It also shows the strike price (110,115, 120), the contract month and year, and if the option is a Call or Put. (C or P)

Bid (pts)

The bid price happens to be the price offered specifically by a market maker to purchase a specific option. Therefore, if you place a market order to dispose of the Call, then you will dispose of it at the bid price indicated.

Ask (pts)

The latest price that a market maker introduces to sell an option is known as the asking price. Therefore, when you are trading options at an options exchange, you get the asking price anytime you ask for the market order. When you purchase options at the bid price or dispose of options with the asking price, you provide market makers with an income. It is recommended that a trader should consider the bid and asking price just before trading. The fact is that active options have tighter bids and ask Spreads compared to less active ones.

The Extrinsic Bid/Ask (pts)

The quantity of time premium that is injected into the option price is displayed in this column. You need to note that all options ultimately lose their time premium as soon as the option expires. Therefore, the extrinsic bid or ask price indicates the total time value that an option has.

Delta Bid/Ask (%)

Delta is derived from a different pricing model. It represents an option's stock equivalent position. Delta values usually range from zero to 100 for Call options, while they range from zero to -100 for Put options.

Gamma Bid/Ask (%)

Just like Delta, Gamma is a Greek value. This value is similarly derived from yet another option pricing model. It gives you information about the number of Deltas that an option stands to lose or gain if the underlying stock goes up by a single point.

Vega Bid/Ask (pts/% IV)

The Vega value shows the amount of expected rise or fall in the price of an option.

This rise and fall would only be based on a single point increase in the stock's volatility. As a trader, you should look to purchase options when the IV or implied volatility is low and then write options when the implied volatility is higher. This way, you will pay a lower time premium.

Volume

This column simply indicates the number of contracts that were traded concerning a particular option. Bids and ask Spreads are often tighter with large volumes, though not all the time.

Strike Price

In options, the strike price is generally the price at which a buyer of an option gets to pay for its underlying security.

Therefore, if a trader wants to exercise their right to purchase the security, the strike price is the price to watch out for.

Important Points to Keep in Mind

The above information is concerning Call options. A Put options table would be almost similar to the one above, save for a couple of differences. You should understand these differences, so you know how to apply them.

Call Options

Call options are costlier when the strike price is lower. On the other hand, Put options are costlier if the strike price is higher. For Call options, the options will have the best or highest prices with lower strike prices. It is also true for Put options where the prices are low with a higher strike level. The reasons for these circumstances are that every strike price is always either more out-of-the-money or less in-the-money. It is inverse with Put options because when the strike prices increase, they become either more in-the-money or less out-of-the-money.

Delta Values

Again, with Call options, Delta values increase at the low strike price and positive. When it comes to Put options, Delta values increase with higher strike prices and are negative. Therefore, when you purchase a Put option, you get a negative Delta value because it resembles a short position.

Make Money with Options Spreading

One of the most common ways of making money with options is through options Spreading. This process typically involves the simultaneous purchase and sale of options. It is where the term Spreading comes in.

Options Spreading also refers to the purchase of options combinations. It is important to understand this concept because it is among the most crucial strategies to earn you plenty of cash repeatedly.

Let us examine options Spreading closely.

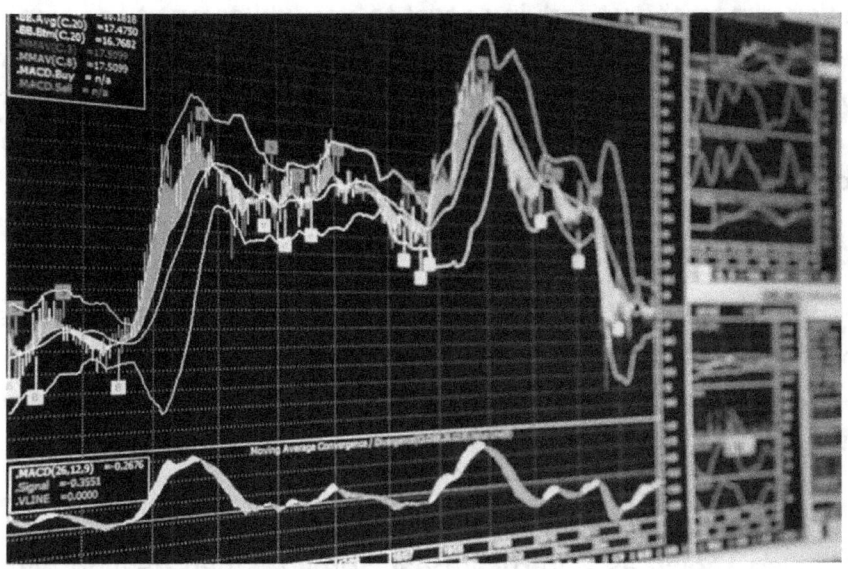

Long Puts and Long Calls

Several option positions are commonly used. The simplest of them all is either a Long Put or a Long Call on its own.

- You stand to benefit greatly from this position if the underlying asset's price and the downside remain limited to the premium.

- A Straddle is created when you simultaneously purchase Put options with a similar strike price and expiration date. You will enjoy huge rewards if there is a rise or fall of the underlying asset's price. The only problem is that you get to lose money should the price remain relatively stable.

- We also have a strategy known as Strangling. It is a strategy employed to purchase a Call option and then a Put option that has a lower strike. It is this Put with a lower strike that gives this strategy its name, Strangle. For this strategy to be successful, then a large price movement either way is necessary.

- When you are Short with either Strangle or Straddle strategies, you will make good money in a market with minimal movement—being Short means that you hope that the asset's price remains in a range for as long as the expiration period is left.

  A strategy that often confuses most short-term traders is being long on Calls and short on Puts. This strategy, also Called "Bull Put Spread," is employed when you expect the underlying asset to rise while you at the same time expect to maximize your profits by being short on Put options. This strategy's two components are: (1) buying Calls with a lower strike than the current stock price and (2) writing a contract with a higher strike than the current stock price but still lower than your premium.

Options Spread Butterflies and Bulls

There are yet other trading strategies that are crucial for successful traders. These also have great potential and will guide you in making large amounts of money. These will essentially show you how to work with certain Spreads. We can have a Call or Put Spread created.

Put Spread

This Spread is also known as a Vertical Bear Spread. When dealing with this option type, you will buy a Put option and then sell another Put option with a lower strike price.

Call Spread

This kind of Spread is also known as the Vertical Bull Spread. You can create this Spread option if you purchase a Call option and at the same time sell a Call option that has a larger strike price. You can profit from this kind of trade when there is an increase in the underlying asset price.

Calendar Spread

Anytime you buy and then sell options with varying expiration dates, these options are referred to as Calendar Spreads. It can also be called a Time Spread.

Butterflies

We can say that we have a Butterfly Spread when there exist options at three distinct strikes. These three strikes are equidistant to each other, and the options at these points are all of a similar kind. It means they are either all Puts or Calls and have a similar expiration time.

We can have either a Short or Long Butterfly. When we have a Long Butterfly case, you should sell the middle strike option and then purchase the outside strikes. These are often bought at the ratio of 1:2:1. It simply means buy one, sell two and then buy another one. This ratio should hold at all times; otherwise, the situation will not be a Butterfly.

The two outside strikes that we mentioned are regularly referred to as the Butterfly's wings, while the inside is known as the body. One important factor that you need to keep in mind is that the Butterfly's value will never get zero.

Butterfly Spread Example

Let us look at an example involving the Butterfly Spread option. We will go Long on a 70 Call, then two Short at 75, and then go Long again with an 80 Call option. We could opt for the two Short 75 Puts, the Long 70 Put, and 80 Put options for our identical trade. Since the Butterfly formation is Long, it will likely benefit from a market with little activity.

Using the Spread example, we can create a synthetic position directly from the options. This kind of strategy is also referred to as the Put-Call parity. Simply Put:

The Call Price – Put Price = Underlying Price – Strike Price

We can use the formula indicated above to come up with a synthetic Long Call. It is by simply rearranging it. Synthetic Puts are simply a combination of a Long Call and short with the underlying security. There are numerous ways of combining all sorts of Spreads with trade in the underlying stocks. By doing this, you will achieve many novel positions like risk reversal, fence, or even Collar. These offer you numerous ways of making money.

CHAPTER 12:

The Risk of Investing or Not Investing

No matter how many safeguards you put in place with your Trading, you will find that there is going to be some risks, and if you are working with swing trading, you will find that there are even more risks with this kind of trading than with some of the other options due to the smaller time frame for the trading. Effectively managing your risks can make a big difference in how successful all of your trades will be. There are four main things that you can do to help you limit your risks and protect your capital, and they include:

- Learn how to assess the risk and the reward of each trade properly

- Set up your stops and your targets

- Manage the dollar size of each trade

- Maintain a journal that has all of your trading activities to help measure your performance and find ways to improve it in the future

Assessing the Risk and the Reward for Each Trade

The first thing that you need to focus on with each of your trades is how to manage your risk. The objective here is not to buy and sell stocks; it is to profit in the stock market. Your broker is the only winner if you go in and randomly buy and sell stocks in the market without any thought of how you will do this. Your job as a trader is to learn how to manage both your risk and your account. Whenever you click on the buy or the sell button, you will expose your money to the loss risk. Figuring out how to limit this a little bit can make a big difference in how much you can earn.

An unsuccessful trader will likely look at an entry and then only think about the profit they will make on that trade. But a successful trader is always going to consider the upside and the downside with any trade they choose. They will think about how much of a risk they will have if they take a loss. It is all about comparing the amount of risk you will take to the reward you hope to get from that trade.

To help you get a good trade setup, you should expect to get at least two times the reward when you compare to the risk you plan to take. If you can get this number higher up, the reward is even better. If you use this strategy with your trading, you will find that you can be successful, even when you are wrong a few times.

Setting Your Stops and Targets

Now that we have a little better idea of the concept of risk to reward, the next thing we need to take a look at is how to put all of this into action. The Stop loss is very important no matter what kind of trading you work with, but it becomes even more important when working with swing trading, and you want to preserve your capital. As a successful trader or someone hoping to become successful, you need to see this stop loss as your best friend.

Any trading system or strategy will end up with losses at some point. A successful trader will keep these losses, and then, they will be able to walk away from a trade that didn't make them a profit. Once you have gone through and done a complete assessment of trade, you have figured out that the potential reward is at least two times the risks; you will then push the right buttons to complete the trade.

Once the trade is started, your capital is now going to be at risk, and the best way to protect it is to set the stop-loss price. This stop point will be the price level where you determine that the trade is going against your predictions, and you want to make sure that you don't lose too much. The place you put this stop loss will depend on the trading strategy that you choose to go with, but it basically will help you go with a small loss rather than the potential big loss that could happen.

Stop-loss is a good way to keep your ego and your emotions out of the game. You have to learn as a trader that the market is right, even if it is going against the predictions you make. You can't control the market; you can only try to predict where it will go. If you are sitting there rationalizing the trade or looking for some justification on why the market isn't moving the way you want it to, emotions have gotten in the way, and you are in trouble.

Manage the Size of the Trade

The next thing that we need to take a look at is managing and controlling how much of your available capital you will invest in one particular trade. Even with a great strategy and a lot of planning, you have times when you have winning trades and times when you will have losing trades. It is why it is important never to overcommit your capital on one trade, or you may work yourself out of the market.

Many experienced traders will use a rule of thumb that says that, for one trade, you should not risk more than two percent of your capital. It means that if you put $20,000 in your account, then you shouldn't risk more than $400 on the trade.

Maintaining a Trading Journal

You can do this online or keep a paper copy nearby. When you are done with one trade, make sure to write down what happened during that trade, what strategy you used, what was going on in the market, how much you spent, etc.

It is a step that many people like to skip, but it can help you out later on. The more details that you can add to it, the better it is. If you ever get stuck with one of your trades or aren't sure how to handle one situation or another, you can refer back to this journal and see what advice it has. You may be surprised that, after a particularly hard situation in a different trade, you can look back in this journal and find the answers you need.

CHAPTER 13:

Answers to Frequently Asked Questions about Option Trading

How Do Put Options Work?

You can purchase Put options contracts through a company in augmentations of 100 offers. (Non-standard options regularly fluctuate from the 100 addition.)

Suppose you consider shares ABC innovation organization will decay inside a quarter of a year from the $100 an offer they are trading today. A Put choice gives you the privilege to sell at your strike cost of $100 inside those three months, regardless of whether the offer value falls beneath that sum.

Accept you practice your Put alternative when the stock tumbles to $90, your income is $10 per share, increased by 100 offers, or $1,000.

Your options contract charges a premium of $2 an offer, you'll have to deduct $200 ($2 x 100 offers) from your benefit, carrying your benefit to $800, less any commissions your financier may charge.

Expert tip: At the point when the cost of your hidden stock falls beneath, make back the initial investment (the strike value less the value you paid); it is gainful (barring commissions).

However, if the stock's value rises, your Put options could be useless, and there's no reason for practicing it. In this circumstance, you'll endure a loss since you'll be out of the $200 premium you paid for the Put options contract.

The above is known as a Long Put methodology.

Similar to Call options, straightforward procedures exist for Put options. And, it's entirely expected to consolidate them with Call options, different Put options, as well as value places that you as of now hold.

A portion of the more typical systems incorporate Stripped Puts, Secured Puts, Put Spreads, Defensive Puts. A Defensive Put (otherwise called a Wedded Put) gives you options to shield the protections you possess from value decreases. In what capacity? You keep on clinging to your offers while also having Put options, which can be thought of as a protection arrangement against value decays.

What occurs if the stock's cost per offer increments? Accept a similar tech stock ascents of $90 per share. That is $20 per share more than your strike cost, so you wouldn't have any desire to practice your Put choice—you'd recently allowed it to lapse.

However, since you purchased the options contract, you'll lose the $300 premium paid: $1 per offer duplicated by 300 offers. Rather, you will be selling your stock, netting you a benefit of $4,200. ($15 duplicated by 300 offers, less the top-notch cost of $300).

Since the potential development of a stock is boundless, you can say that the potential benefit of a secured Put is likewise boundless, short the premium paid.

Differences Between Covered and Naked Puts

Naked and Covered Puts become an integral factor when you're the dealer. A Put is viewed as secured if you likewise short the equal number of offers in the fundamental security. Shorting the fundamental stock is the point at which you get offers and promptly sell them, trusting that you can get them again later at a less expensive cost.

Expert tip: A secured Put is a system to consider if you accept a stock's cost will fall.

Then again, if you figure a stock's cost will stay unaltered or will rise, you might need to think about an exposed Put alternative (or revealed Put, or Short Put). With a Naked Put, you don't short portions of the hidden stock.

With a Naked Put, if you get the fundamental protections, they will be at the strike cost. Here are how a stripped Put works.

Keep in mind the ABC tech organization? Suppose you think the stock will remain leveled or go up, so you sell a Naked Put option with a strike cost of $90. In return for tolerating the commitment to purchase 100 portions of XYZ at $90, if XYZ dips under the strike value, you get a premium option of $1 an offer, or $100. If the offer cost is over the strike cost of $90/share and its option terminates, you keep the options premium you got, and you are eased of your commitment.

Genius tip: The principle objective of Naked Put options trading is to gather the options premium as salary, so you would prefer not to use this technique if you think the stock's cost is drifting descending.

It's an alternate situation if the basic stock value falls beneath $90. In principle, the cost could go right to zero, and you would be committed to purchase 100 portions of XYZ at the strike cost of $90.

Comparison between Put Options and Short Selling

Purchasing Puts is like short selling in that you're wagering against a stock, yet they're not a similar sort of exchange.

A few investors lean toward trading options because you don't have to obtain security, as you do with short deals. Furthermore, the drawback to Put options is topped at the sum you spend purchasing the agreement. Keep in mind:

The purchaser of the Put options has a right, yet not a commitment, to sell the stock if they have a Put option. So regardless of whether they misjudge and the stock ascents, they are just out the premium.

Short selling is diverse even though your losses can keep on mounting until you purchase the stock to close the position.

Risks Associated with Put Options

As we referenced, Put options can be an approach to improve your profit during a down market (or notwithstanding during a solitary security's downturn). In any case, options trading isn't for novice investors. Of course, it can give adaptability, openings, and a degree of risk decrease; however, options dealing itself isn't without risk.

Self-coordinated or do-it-without anyone's help, investors should initially gain proficiency with the intricate details of options dealing before hopping in.

One risk involved is time decay. Every day, the estimation of your options is rotted by time. At the end of the day, the closer your agreement gets to its lapse date, the less time there is for the security to move one way or the other.

Genius tip: One procedure to moderate time rot is to use longer options contracts of three to a half years or sell your agreement the closer you get to the termination date.

Another risk is suggested instability, which shows how unstable the market could be later on. In case you're attempting to make sense of the opportunity of a stock achieving a particular cost by a specific time, suggested instability can enable you to gain entry into an options trade with full knowledge of the market's feeling.

Volatility: It is the sum a stock cost changes—is likewise another such risk.

While some fear a descending turn in the market, Put options can be a route for bearish investors to exploit descending value moves. They're not without risk, yet they can be the silver covering in a drooping financial market.

Conclusion

Remember that risk management is paramount. Always stick to your per-trade risk figures and do not deviate from this, no matter how attractive the setup might seem. Remember, the odds of success of a slam-dunk-looking setup and one that looks like a dog's dinner is the same. The market does not care about how pretty your setup is, so neither should you. If the underlying conditions are fulfilled, you should correctly execute your setup.

Your analysis should always begin with the technical market situation: the order flow distribution and the trend or range situation. Often you will deal with trends with close to equal participation from both sides of the market. It should tell you that a reversal is probably imminent, and you should adjust accordingly.

Support and resistance will play an important role in determining where you ought to place your strike prices. Remember to evaluate support and resistance levels from an order flow perspective instead of looking at every single available level on the chart. Look at how the order flow characteristics of the preceding time price made it there and compare it to the current order flow to get a feel for whether the level will hold or not.

Screening stocks is a straightforward matter if you follow the process outlined here. Compare the sector performance to the overall market performance to narrow down which sectors you should focus on. Once this is done, repeat the same process with individual stocks to select the best to speculate with.

Training and ending up with a loss or paying for training and earning profits? Well, it is entirely up to you to decide. I can say that having a mentor will prevent you from incurring unnecessary losses and result in a positive outcome.

Now that you are well equipped with the necessary information, it's about time that you kick-start your journey in options trading. It is a good investment that can end with a favorable outcome. You know what it entails, its pros and cons, the option strategies and tips for success; what else are you waiting for to start investing? You should be in the process of opening a brokerage account as you start your journey as an options trader. It is currently the 'coolest' investment to start trading. Life comes with endless opportunities, and options trading happens to be one of them. If you are looking for an investment that will completely transform your life, this is it. It is a convenient, reliable, and fantastic way to generate an income. Some people have made it a full-time investment. They have identified it as an investment that they can rely on for a successful outcome. If you are new to options trading, this is a perfect investment to carry out. The trick is to master the tactics that will increase your returns and minimize the risks. After all, the whole point of investing is to earn profits.

There are a lot of different types of investments out there that you can choose to work with. Some are going to include taking over real estate and renting it out or selling it to somebody else. Some will get into their own business and try to make money that way. And still, others will get into the stock market and hope they can make the right decisions. But one investment that is different from all the others is options trading.

This guidebook has taken some time to talk about options trading and all the neat things you can do with it. We talked a bit about options and some of the benefits of choosing to work with them.

As with any investment type, there is some risk involved when you get into options trading. The good news is that we spent some time talking about the most common mistakes to avoid and how to reduce the amount of risk that you take on inside this investment opportunity. Options investing is a tricky investment to choose to go with, but it provides a great return on investment and is often easier to get into compared to the stock market

It is a good idea to put all of this into a trading plan to summarize your market approach. Think of it as your trading business plan for success. List your instruments to trade, which strategies you will follow, and how you will expand on them.

The topics covered here only scratch the surface with regards to trading options. There are a lot more strategies to consider. Your subsequent step would be to learn the Greeks and to apply them in strategies. I am not talking about the Iliad but the letters Delta, Theta, Omega, Alpha, and Beta. You can also learn about ratio back Spreads and Butterfly trades. All of this sounds very exotic, but they are extremely effective.

However, before proceeding, you should master the material here. The biggest problem for most traders is adjusting to the non-directional aspect of options. Understanding a stop loss and taking profit is easy, but dealing with a Call option and a Short Put while experiencing a falling market tends to spin people's heads.

From novice to initiated, you have now gained the basics of knowledge that will help you enter the exciting world of options trading. It certainly is not everything there is to know, but you now have enough grounding to get started.

From here out, it is all about practice and being conservative as you improve your understanding and develop your strategies. Only you will know what works best for you, how much risk you want to play with, and how your personal ability to predict and determine the stock market can be best put into practice.

As you dip your feet into the water, you will start to see profits coming in, and you will feel that buzz all options traders enjoy.

You are in for a treat—options trading is rewarding and exciting when done right. Remember to keep that calendar updated and stay conservative initially, and you will enjoy that learning curve every step of the way!

Do not let one loss get you discouraged. The wealthiest traders and investors have all taken hits from which they thought they would never recover from. Remember that you will have a few moments where you don't get as much back as you hoped, but know that you will also have moments where you make more money than you ever did with your initial investment.

You have now had a careful stroll through the key standards and ventures in options trading we feel are fundamental to progress as an options trader. You have figured out how the options markets functions, the best trading strategies and why it is basic to pick the best possible fundamental assets for the procedures you need to utilize.

You have additionally observed that great exit strategies are nearly as imperative as discovering great trades to enter, that focusing on the points of interest is basic. That achievement is virtually inconceivable without a decent money-management plan—and the discipline to follow it.

At last, you have got lots of pages loaded with vital inquiries to consider in your search for the best online options broker. It is a great opportunity to control up, plugin—and profit. You have all the data to appreciate 24-hour access to the options markets, fast and programmed execution of your orders, and the most reduced commissions in the history of options trading. In any case, to share these advantages, you should confront the bigger individual duties that accompany coordinated access to online trading.

You should have the discipline to do your very own research, screen your positions, and monitor every one of the points of interest you may leave to your full-benefit financial firm. You can never again depend on a broker to watch your positions and Call with guidance or suggestions. You are currently an *autonomous administrator*—and must be absolutely in charge of your behavior.

Likewise, you should be mindful and be prepared to react to both fast moves in every trading designs and consistently evolving longer-term economic situations.

Thank you for reading this through to the end! I hope that you have found this to be informative and educational.

Options are a great way to get in the stock market with a lot less upfront capital. They can be tricky because they come with expiration dates, so you must get in and out at the right time and cannot wait things out like you can with a stock.

But the return on investment is far superior to stocks when you make profitable trades. Be sure to study the securities that you are investing in carefully to know where the stock has real potential to move.

Also, keep learning, and I hope this was a good start.